GLOBE QUARTOS

KING LEIR

First printed: London, 1605

This edition prepared by Tiffany Stern

GLOBE EDUCATION

and

A Theatre Arts Book

Routledge
Taylor & Francis Group
NEW YORK

GLOBE QUARTOS

This edition of *King Leir*
first published in Great Britain
as a paperback original in 2002
by Nick Hern Books Limited
14 Larden Road, London W3 7ST

Published in the United States and Canada in 2003
by Theatre Arts Books/Routledge
29 West 35th Street
New York, NY 10001
www.routledge-ny.com
Routledge is an imprint of the Taylor & Francis Group

in association with

Globe Education
Shakespeare's Globe, New Globe Walk
London SE1 9DT

A CIP catalogue record for this book is available from
the Library of Congress

ISBN 0-87830-160-7

PREFACE

Over 400 plays written between 1567 and 1642 have survived in print. Few are now read and even fewer are performed. In 1995 Globe Education initiated a 30-year project to stage readings with professional casts of all the surviving texts so that audiences may once again hear plays by Barnes, Haughton, Shirley, Wilkins *et al.*

In 1997 Mark Rylance, Artistic Director of Shakespeare's Globe, included full productions of Beaumont and Fletcher's *The Maid's Tragedy* and Middleton's *A Chaste Maid in Cheapside* as part of the Globe Theatre's opening season. Over 30,000 people came to hear and see the two plays.

The popularity of the readings and the productions prompted Globe Education to approach Nick Hern to publish the texts being revived at the Globe to enable more people to read, study and, ideally, to produce them. The first *Globe Quartos* were edited in 1998 by Nick de Somogyi. In 1999 an Editorial Board, composed of David Scott Kastan, Gordon McMullan and Richard Proudfoot, was established to oversee the series.

Globe Education is indebted to all those who have helped to give new life to old plays: production teams, actors, audiences, directors, editors, publishers and readers.

Patrick Spottiswoode
Director, Globe Education

EDITORIAL BOARD'S PREFACE

The aim of the series is to make once more available English plays of the late sixteenth and early seventeenth centuries that have long been out of print in affordable form or have been available to readers only in scholarly editions in academic libraries. The *Globe Quartos* texts are based on the most reliable surviving forms of these plays (usually the first printed editions). These have been fully edited and modernised so as to make them easily usable by actors and readers today. Editorial correction and emendation are undertaken where required by the state of the original. Extra stage directions added by editors and needed to make the action clear are enclosed in square brackets. Apostrophes in verse speeches indicate elision of syllables and reflect the metrical pattern of the line. Prefatory matter includes notes form the director or co-ordinator of the production or reading of the play at the Globe and a brief factual introduction by the editor. Glossarial notes (keyed to the text by line numbers) explain difficult or obsolete usages and offer brief comment on other points of interest or obscurity. Departures from the wording of the original are recorded in textual notes that identify the source of corrections or editorial emendations. The opening page of the text in the original on which the edition is based is reproduced in reduced facsimile. Extra material relevant to the understanding of the play may occasionally be included in an Appendix.

A NOTE FROM THE CO-ORDINATOR

From the first reading, I was intrigued by the curious miscellany of styles in *Leir*. There is the saucy knockabout stuff and the thundering fustian – and then all of a sudden it becomes easy and charming. The mixture of grandiloquence and comedy, interspersed with touching scenes (particularly those between Leir and Perillus) shows the theatrical instincts of the anonymous author and certainly gives great opportunities to actors. In performance the comic scenes went down very well. I was surprised to discover how much humour there is in the roles of both the French Ambassador and the Murderer – though perhaps these laughs were a tribute more to the timing and skills of Philip Franks and David Michaels than to the craft of the anonymous author. Another unexpected success was the characterisation of the two Ugly Sisters, whom the audience immediately recognised as straight out of Panto, provoking several bold hisses and boos. Everyone thoroughly enjoyed it, and there was a kind of indulgent fondness in their reactions: 'How sweet, isn't he writing well – considering ...' The truth is that none of us present could watch this version of the Lear myth without being constantly mindful of what Shakespeare did with it. I imagined him watching this clunky old war-horse and having the talent not just to laugh at it, but to take it and reforge it. Anyone can mock; it takes great intuition to see and extract what is pathetical. And because, finally, *Leir* remains an apologue, never venturing into the wild and frightening territory of Shakespeare's *Lear*, there is a tendency to condescend to its anonymous writer – yet the reaction of the audience at the end of *Leir* proved how deep within us runs the desire for a restitution of some order, some moral orthodoxy, a desire which of course Shakespeare wilfully frustrates. His *Lear* is certainly a greater play, but not always a more enjoyable one.

Jonathan Cullen

ACKNOWLEDGEMENTS

I would like to thank all those whose help made this edition possible, in particular earlier editors of the play. I am deeply grateful to Gordon McMullan for his scholarly and personal help, as well as for giving me *Leir* in the first place; David Scott Kastan's invaluable comments and suggestions prevented the play from becoming, as he feared, 'a ship without a stern'. Other people deserve acknowledgement for living with me while I was working on *Leir* in Poland and in England. They are Elspeth Findlay, Samuel Kessler and Kerensa Heffron. Alas, they do not include Artur Ekert, to whom this edition is, with love, dedicated.

Tiffany Stern

KING LEIR

Cast of the staged reading at Globe Education, Beargardens, 22 July 2001, co-ordinated by Jonathan Cullen

King Leir	Bernard Gallagher
Skalliger	Philip Franks
Noble	Jonathan Cullen
Perillus	Patrick Godfrey
King of Gallia	Declan Conlon
Lord Mumford	Sam Callis
The King of Cornwall	James Simmons
Prince of Cambria	Ronan Vibert
Servant to King of Cornwall	Jonathan Cullen
Messenger	David Michaels
Gallian Ambassador	Philip Franks
First Mariner	David Michaels
Second Mariner	Philip Franks
Captain of the Watch	Jonathan Cullen
Watchman One	David Michaels
Watchman Two	Philip Franks
Chief of the Town	Jonathan Cullen

Gonorill	Elaine Claxton
Ragan	Gillian Bevan
Cordella	Sally Ann Burnett

Nobles, Captains and Attendants played by members of the Company

EDITOR'S INTRODUCTION

Although the earliest surviving editions of the anonymous *King Leir* date from 1605, the play has an older heritage. Philip Henslowe, who kept a daily record of plays performed in his Rose Playhouse, received receipts for a *kinge leare* on 6 April 1594. That play was performed again two days later 'by the Quenes men and my lord of Sussexe to geather', and licensed for publication in the same year: a Stationers' Company Record of May 14 1594 allows one Edward White the right to publish 'a booke entituled The moste famous Chronicle historye of Leire kinge of England and his Three Daughters'. The problem is that no copies exist from 1594: either none has survived or, as seems likely, *Leir* was not in fact printed then for some reason. But the result is that we cannot be certain whether the text published in 1605 is that of the earlier *Leir*, of a newly revised edition, or possibly of a different play altogether. Its licence in the Stationers' Company Register is itself odd: the new entry of May 8 1605 is assigned first to Simon Stafford, then to John Wright ('provided that Simon Stafford shall haue the printinge of this booke'), with no mention made of the fact that White had ownership of the text. That 1605 play, published by John Wright, printed by Simon Stafford, and described as having been 'latelie Acted', is the text printed in this edition.

A number of playwrights have been put forward as possible authors for *Leir* – Marlowe, Lodge, Kyd, Peele, Greene, William Rankins (writer of several historical plays for Henslowe, all of which are lost), or the same anonymous writer responsible for *Locrine* – but the play does not clearly recall the style of any one particular playwright from the period. Modern textual scholars have shown that a large number and variety of authors worked for and in playhouses and, as a result, 'attribution studies' themselves are now coming into question: further thought on the authorship of *Leir* seems futile here. What we can be more sure about are the sources the playwright used. The Lear legend had been popular ever since first recorded by Geoffrey of Monmouth in his Latin history of British kings, *Historia regium Britanniae* (c. 1135); by the time *Leir* was written, the story had been retold by over fifty writers, historians, and poets. The author of the *Leir* play, however, shows a particular knowledge of certain texts – William Warner's *Albion's England* (1586), John Higgins's additions to *The Mirror for Magistrates* (1574) and Spenser's *Faerie Queen* (1590). To the story they tell, he adds three important characters, all of them counsellors: the trusty Perillus, the disingenuous Scaliger, and a comic Frenchman with the unlikely name of 'Mumford'. In addition he creates a saucy wooing scene between Cordella and the Gallian King, a scene in which a hired killer (called simply 'Messenger') attempts to murder Leir and Perillus, and a reconciliation scene between Leir, Cordella, the King and Mumford. This is a gentle, humorous, and unquestioningly Christian rendering of the Leir tale, ending at the moment when Gonoril and Ragan have lost the battle, and the crown has been successfully won back for Leir. 'Thanks be to God,' exclaims the Gallian King, 'your foes are overcome / And you again possessed of your right.' Leir then gives his crown to Cordella and the Gallian King, enjoining them to 'Repose with me awhile and then for France'.

It is hard to determine how well Shakespeare knew *Leir*. He was, it has recently been suggested, a player in the Queen's company of the 1590s; if that were the case, he may actually have performed in the play. But there are many other ways in which he could have become familiar with *Leir*. He could have seen it performed, read it in manuscript, or simply been told about it. There are few close verbal parallels between the two texts, but key moments in Shakespeare's *Lear* are tragic reworkings of what is often comic or semi-comic in *Leir*. So Leir's elderly eccentricity becomes Lear's madness; Perillus's humanity, wisdom and friendship become Kent's bluffness and the Fool's cold truths; the farcical kneeling and rising of Cordella, Leir, the Gallian King and Mumford become the heart-breaking reconciliation scene between the newly-sane Lear and Cordelia. Perhaps, most chillingly, what in *Leir* is a divine thunder-clap sent to redeem the Messenger from his murderous intent is in *Lear* seemingly a proof of the cruelty or non-existence of God, bespeaking the 'horrible pleasure' of the elements in attacking 'a poor, infirm, weak, and despis'd old man' at his lowest ebb. Much depends on when Shakespeare wrote his play – but even that cannot be strictly determined. The first performance of Shakespeare's *Lear* on record is for a court production on December 26 1606, a year after the publication of *Leir* – but Shakespeare's text may have been written some time before that. He may, indeed, have been stimulated by seeing a new production of the old play or by reading the 1605 edition; alternatively, as is sometimes suggested, the anonymous *Leir* may have been printed in order to exploit interest in Shakespeare's *Lear* (or even in order to gull potential readers into thinking they were buying Shakespeare's play).

Whatever the nature of the connection, *Leir* is a source for Shakespeare, and in reading it we can see the raw material that Shakespeare was inspired to work on. Four copies of the 1605 quarto have survived. Two are collated in the *Malone Society Reprint* of 1908, which forms the basis of this text.

Tiffany Stern

KING
LEIR

DRAMATIS PERSONAE

The Persons in the Play

LEIR	*King of Britain*
SCALLIGER NOBLEMAN } PERILLUS	*courtiers of Leir*
GONORIL RAGAN } CORDELLA	*daughters of Leir*
The King of GALLIA	*suitor and then husband of Cordella*
MUMFORD	*Gallia's man*
The King of CORNWALL	*suitor and then husband of Gonoril*
His Man	
Morgan, King of CAMBRIA	*suitor and then husband of Regan*
His Man	
MESSENGER *from Cornwall*	*Messenger and would-be murderer*
AMBASSADOR *of Gallia*	
1 MARINER 2 MARINER 1 WATCHMAN } 2 WATCHMAN 1 CAPTAIN 2 CAPTAIN	
French NOBLES	
British NOBLEMAN	
Chief of Town	
Attendants, Soldiers, Townsfolk	

[1.1]

Enter King LEIR[, SCALIGER, PERILLUS] *and* [NOBLEMAN]

Leir   Thus, to our grief, the obsequies perform'd
                Of our too late deceas'd and dearest queen,
                Whose soul, I hope, possess'd of heavenly joys,
                Doth ride in triumph 'mongst the cherubims,
                Let us request your grave advice, my lords,
                For the disposing of our princely daughters,
                For whom our care is specially employ'd,
                As nature bindeth, to advance their states
                In royal marriage with some princely mates.
                For wanting now their mother's good advice,   10
                Under whose government they have receiv'd
                A perfect pattern of a virtuous life,
                Left as it were a ship without a stern
                Or silly sheep without a pastor's care,
                Although ourselves do dearly tender them,
                Yet are we ignorant of their affairs;
                For fathers best do know to govern sons,
                But daughters' steps the mother's counsel turns.
                A son we want for to succeed our crown,
                And course of time hath cancelled the date   20
                Of further issue from our wither'd loins.
                One foot already hangeth in the grave,
                And age hath made deep furrows in my face.
                The world of me, I of the world am weary,
                And I would fain resign these earthly cares,
                And think upon the welfare of my soul,
                Which by no better means may be effected
                Than by resigning up the crown from me
                In equal dowry to my daughters three.

Scaliger	A worthy care, my liege, which well declares 30
	The zeal you bare unto our quondam queen.
	And since your grace hath licens'd me to speak,
	I censure thus: your majesty knowing well
	What several suitors your princely daughters have,
	To make them each a jointure – more or less
	As is their worth – to them that love profess.
Leir	No more nor less, but even all alike.
	My zeal is fix'd: all fashion'd in one mould,
	Wherefore unpartial shall my censure be;
	Both old and young shall have alike from me. 40
Nobleman	My gracious lord, I heartily do wish
	That God had lent you an heir indubitate –
	Which might have sat upon your royal throne
	When fates should loose the prison of your life –
	By whose succession all this doubt might cease
	And, as by you, by him we might have peace.
	But after-wishes ever come too late,
	And nothing can revoke the course of fate:
	Wherefore, my liege, my censure deems it best
	To match them with some of your neighbour kings, 50
	Bord'ring within the bounds of Albion,
	By whose united friendship, this our state
	May be protected 'gainst all foreign hate.
Leir	Herein, my lords, your wishes sort with mine,
	And mine, I hope, do sort with heav'nly powers:
	For at this instant two near-neighbouring kings
	Of Cornwall and of Cambria motion love
	To my two daughters, Gonoril and Ragan.
	My youngest daughter, fair Cordella, vows
	No liking to a monarch, unless love allows. 60
	She is solicited by divers peers,

But none of them her partial fancy hears.
Yet, if my policy may her beguile,
I'll match her to some king within this isle
And so establish such a perfect peace
As Fortune's force shall ne'er prevail to cease.

Perillus   Of us and ours your gracious care, my lord,
Deserves an everlasting memory
To be enroll'd in chronicles of fame
By never-dying perpetuity;   70
Yet to become so provident a prince,
Lose not the title of a loving father:
Do not force love where fancy cannot dwell,
Lest streams, being stopp'd, above the banks do swell.

Leir   I am resolv'd, and even now my mind
Doth meditate a sudden stratagem
To try which of my daughters loves me best,
Which, till I know, I cannot be in rest.
This granted, when they jointly shall contend
Each to exceed the other in their love,   80
Then at the vantage will I take Cordella
Even as she doth protest she loves me best,
I'll say: 'Then, daughter, grant me one request
To show thou lov'st me as thy sisters do:
Accept a husband whom myself will woo'.
This said, she cannot well deny my suit,
Although, poor soul, her senses will be mute.
Then will I triumph in my policy
And match her with a king of Brittany.   89

Scaliger   [*aside*] I'll to them before, and bewray your secrecy.

Perillus   [*aside*] Thus fathers think their children to beguile,
And oftentimes themselves do first repent

When heav'nly powers do frustrate their intent.   *Exeun*

Enter GONORIL *and* RAGAN

Gonoril   I marvel, Ragan, how you can endure
To see that proud pert peat, our youngest sister,
So slightly to account of us, her elders,
As if we were no better than herself!
We cannot have a quaint device so soon
Or new-made fashion of our choice invention,
But, if she like it, she will have the same
Or study newer to exceed us both.
Besides, she is so nice and so demure,
So sober, courteous, modest and precise   10
That all the court hath work enough to do
To talk how she exceedeth me and you.

Ragan   What should I do? Would it were in my power
To find a cure for this contagious ill!
Some desp'rate medicine must be soon applied
To dim the glory of her mounting fame
Else, ere't be long, she'll have both prick and praise,
And we must be set by for working days.
Do you not see what several choice of suitors
She daily hath, and of the best degree?   20
Say amongst all she hap to fancy one
And have a husband whenas we have none;
Why then, by right, to her we must give place,
Though it be ne'er so much to our disgrace.

Gonoril   By my virginity, rather than she shall have

	A husband before me,
	I'll marry one or other in his shirt.
	And yet I have made half a grant already
	Of my good will unto the king of Cornwall. 29
Ragan	Swear not so deeply, sister. Here cometh my lord Scaliger.
	Something his hasty coming doth import.

Enter SCALIGER

Scaliger	Sweet princesses, I am glad I met you here so luckily,
	Having good news which doth concern you both
	And craveth speedy expedition.
Ragan	For God's sake tell us what it is, my lord;
	I am with child until you utter it.
Scaliger	Madam, to save your longing, this it is:
	Your father, in great secrecy, today
	Told me he means to marry you out of hand
	Unto the noble prince of Cambria. 40
	[*To* GONORIL] You, madam, to the king of Cornwall's

grace.

Your younger sister he would fain bestow
Upon the rich king of Hibernia,
But that he doubts she hardly will consent,
For hitherto she ne'er could fancy him.
If she do yield, why then, between you three
He will divide his kingdom for your dowries.
But yet there is a further mystery
Which, so you will conceal, I will disclose.

Gonoril	Whate'er thou speak'st to us, kind Scaliger, 50
	Think that thou speak'st it only to thyself.
Scaliger	He earnestly desireth for to know
	Which of you three do bear most love to him,

And on your loves he so extremely dotes
As never any did, I think, before.
He presently doth mean to send for you
To be resolv'd of this tormenting doubt,
And look whose answer pleaseth him the best,
They shall have most unto their marriages.

Ragan   Oh, that I had some pleasing mermaid's voice   60
            For to enchant his senseless senses with!

Scaliger   For he supposeth that Cordella will,
            Striving to go beyond you in her love,
            Promise to do whatever he desires.
            Then will he straight enjoin her for his sake
            Th'Hibernian king in marriage for to take.
            This is the sum of all I have to say,
            Which, being done, I humbly take my leave,
            Not doubting but your wisdoms will foresee
            What course will best unto your good agree.   70

Gonoril   Thanks, gentle Scaliger; thy kindness undeserved
            Shall not be unrequited, if we live.   Exit SCALIGE

Ragan   Now have we fit occasion offer'd us
            To be reveng'd upon her unperceiv'd.

Gonoril   Nay, our revenge we will inflict on her
            Shall be accounted piety in us.
            I will so flatter with my doting father
            As he was ne'er so flatter'd in his life.
            Nay, I will say that if it be his pleasure
            To match me to a beggar, I will yield.   80
            For why, I know whatever I do say,
            He means to match me with the Cornwall king.

Ragan   I'll say the like, for I am well assur'd

Whate'er I say to please the old man's mind,
Who dotes as if he were a child again,
I shall enjoy the noble Cambrian prince.
Only, to feed his humour, will suffice
To say I am content with anyone
Whom he'll appoint me. This will please him more
Then e'er Apollo's music pleased Jove.   90

Gonoril   I smile to think in what a woeful plight
Cordella will be when we answer thus,
For she will rather die than give consent
To join in marriage with the Irish king.
So will our father think she loveth him not,
Because she will not grant to his desire –
Which we will aggravate in such bitter terms
That he will soon convert his love to hate:
For he, you know, is always in extremes.

Ragan   Not all the world could lay a better plot;   100
I long till it be put in practice.   Exeunt

[1.3]
                    Enter LEIR *and* PERILLUS

Leir   Perillus, go seek my daughters. Will them
Immediately come and speak with me.

Perillus   I will, my gracious lord.   Exit

Leir   Oh, what a combat feels my panting heart
'Twixt children's love and care of common weal!
How dear my daughters are unto my soul
None knows but He that knows my thoughts and secret
                                                          deeds.
Ah, little do they know the dear regard

Wherein I hold their future state to come.
When they securely sleep on beds of down,   10
These aged eyes do watch for their behalf;
While they like wantons sport in youthful toys,
This throbbing heart is pierc'd with dire annoys.
As doth the sun exceed the smallest star,
So much the father's love exceeds the child's.
Yet my complaints are causeless, for the world
Affords not children more conformable –
And yet, methinks, my mind presageth still
I know not what, and yet I fear some ill.

Enter PERILLUS, *with the three daughters* [GONORIL, RAGAN *and*
CORDELLA]

Well, here my daughters come. I have found out   20
A present means to rid me of this doubt.

Gonoril   Our royal lord and father, in all duty
We come to know the tenor of your will,
Why you so hastily have sent for us.

Leir   Dear Gonoril, kind Ragan, sweet Cordella,
Ye flourishing branches of a kingly stock
Sprung from a tree that once did flourish green,
Whose blossoms now are nipp'd with winter's frost,
And pale grim death doth wait upon my steps,
And summons me unto his next assizes –   30
Therefore, dear daughters, as ye tender the safety
Of him that was the cause of your first being,
Resolve a doubt which much molests my mind:
Which of you three to me would prove most kind,
Which loves me most, and which at my request
Will soonest yield unto their father's hest.

Gonoril   I hope my gracious father makes no doubt

Of any of his daughters' love to him.
Yet, for my part, to show my zeal to you,
Which cannot be in windy words rehears'd,   40
I prize my love to you at such a rate,
I think my life inferior to my love.
Should you enjoin me for to tie a millstone
About my neck and leap into the sea,
At your command I willingly would do it.
Yea, for to do you good, I would ascend
The highest turret in all Brittany
And, from the top, leap headlong to the ground.
Nay, more! Should you appoint me for to marry
The meanest vassal in the spacious world,   50
Without reply I would accomplish it.
In brief, command whatever you desire
And, if I fail, no favour I require.

Leir   Oh, how thy words revive my dying soul!

Cordella   [*aside*] Oh, how I do abhor this flattery!

Leir   But what saith Ragan to her father's will?

Ragan   Oh, that my simple utterance could suffice
To tell the true intention of my heart,
Which burns in zeal of duty to your grace
And never can be quench'd but by desire   60
To show the same in outward forwardness.
Oh, that there were some other maid that durst
But make a challenge of her love with me;
I'd make her soon confess she never lov'd
Her father half so well as I do you.
Ay, then my deeds should prove in plainer case
How much my zeal aboundeth to your grace.
But for them all, let this one mean suffice

To ratify my love before your eyes:
I have right noble suitors to my love,   70
No worse than kings, and haply I love one;
Yet, would you have me make my choice anew,
I'd bridle fancy and be ruled by you.

Leir   Did never Philomel sing so sweet a note.

Cordella [*aside*] Did never flatterer tell so false a tale.

Leir   Speak now, Cordella, make my joys at full
And drop down nectar from thy honey lips.

Cordella I cannot paint my duty forth in words;
I hope my deeds shall make report for me:
But look what love the child doth owe the father,   80
The same to you I bear, my gracious lord.

Gonoril   Here is an answer answerless indeed;
Were you my daughter, I should scarcely brook it.

Ragan   Dost thou not blush, proud peacock as thou art,
To make our father such a slight reply?

Leir   Why, how now, minion? Are you grown so proud?
Doth our dear love make you thus peremptory?
What, is your love become so small to us
As that you scorn to tell us what it is?
Do you love us as every child doth love   90
Their father? True, indeed, as some
Who by disobedience short their fathers' days,
And so would you; some are so father-sick
That they make means to rid them from the world,
And so would you; some are indifferent
Whether their aged parents live or die,
And so are you. But, didst thou know, proud girl,
What care I had to foster thee to this,

	Ah, then thou wouldst say, as thy sisters do,	
	'Our life is less than love we owe to you.'	100
Cordella	Dear father, do not so mistake my words,	
	Nor my plain meaning be misconstrued;	
	My tongue was never us'd to flattery.	
Gonoril	You were not best say I flatter: if you do,	
	My deeds shall show I flatter not with you.	
	I love my father better then thou canst.	
Cordella	The praise were great, spoke from another's mouth,	
	But it should seem your neighbours dwell far off.	
Ragan	Nay, here is one that will confirm as much	
	As she hath said, both for myself and her.	110
	I say, thou dost not wish my father's good.	
Cordella	Dear father –	
Leir	Peace, bastard imp, no issue of King Leir!	
	I will not hear thee speak one tittle more.	
	Call not me father if thou love thy life,	
	Nor these thy sisters once presume to name;	
	Look for no help henceforth from me nor mine.	
	Shift as thou wilt and trust unto thyself.	
	My kingdom will I equally divide	
	'Twixt thy two sisters to their royal dower,	120
	And will bestow them worthy their deserts.	
	This done, because thou shalt not have the hope	
	To have a child's part in the time to come,	
	I presently will dispossess myself	
	And set up these upon my princely throne.	
Gonoril	I ever thought that pride would have a fall.	
Ragan	Plain-dealing sister, your beauty is so sheen	

You need no dowry to make you be a queen!

Exeunt LEIR, GONORIL, RAGAN

Cordella   Now 'whither, poor forsaken, shall I go' –
When mine own sisters triumph in my woe –   130
But unto Him which doth protect the just?
In Him will poor Cordella put her trust.
These hands shall labour for to get my spending,
And so I'll live until my days have ending.   [*Exit*]

Perillus   Oh, how I grieve to see my lord thus fond
To dote so much upon vain flattering words.
Ah, if he but with good advice had weigh'd
The hidden tenor of her humble speech,
Reason to rage should not have given place,   139
Nor poor Cordella suffer such disgrace.   *Exit*

[2.1]

Enter the King of GALLIA *with* MUMFORD, *and three* FRENCH NOBLES *more*

Gallia   Dissuade me not, my lords! I am resolv'd
This next fair wind to sail for Brittany
In some disguise, to see if flying fame
Be not too prodigal in the wondrous praise
Of these three nymphs, the daughters of King Leir.
If present view do answer absent praise,
And eyes allow of what our ears have heard,
And Venus stand auspicious to my vows,
And Fortune favour what I take in hand,
I will return seiz'd of as rich a prize   10
As Jason, when he won the golden fleece.

Mumford   Heav'ns grant you may. The match were full of honour
And well beseeming the young Gallian king.
I would your grace would favour me so much
As make me partner of your pilgrimage.
I long to see the gallant British dames
And feed mine eyes upon their rare perfections,
For till I know the contrary, I'll say
Our dames in France are far more fair than they.

Gallia   Lord Mumford, you have saved me a labour   20
In off'ring that which I did mean to ask,
And I most willingly accept your company.
Yet first I will enjoin you to observe
Some few conditions which I shall propose.

Mumford   So that you do not tie mine eyes for looking
After the amorous glances of fair dames;
So that you do not tie my tongue from speaking,

My lips from kissing when occasion serves,
My hands from congés, and my knees to bow
To gallant girls – which were a task more hard   30
Than flesh and blood is able to endure –
Command what else you please, I rest content.

Gallia   To bind thee from a thing thou canst not leave
Were but a mean to make thee seek it more,
And therefore speak, look, kiss, salute for me;
In these myself am like to second thee.
Now hear thy task: I charge thee from the time
That first we set sail for the British shore
To use no words of dignity to me
But, in the friendliest manner that thou canst,   40
Make use of me as thy companion.
For we will go disguised in palmers' weeds
That no man shall mistrust us what we are.

Mumford   If that be all, I'll fit your turn, I warrant you.
I am some kin to the Blunts and, I think, the
bluntest of all my kindred; therefore if I be too
blunt with you, thank yourself for praying me to be so.

Gallia   Thy pleasant company will make the way seem short.
It resteth now that in my absence hence
I do commit the government to you,   50
My trusty lords and faithful counsellors.
Time cuts off the rest I have to say;
The wind blows fair, and I must needs away.

Nobles   Heav'ns send your voyage to as good effect
As we your land do purpose to protect.   *Exeunt*

[2.2]

Enter the King of CORNWALL *booted and spurred, a riding wand and a letter in his hand* [*and* SERVANT]

Cornwall   But how far distant are we from the court?

Servant   Some twenty miles, my lord, or thereabouts.

Cornwall   It seemeth to me twenty thousand miles;
           Yet hope I to be there within this hour.

Servant   (*to himself*) Then are you like to ride alone. For me,
           I think my lord is weary of his life.

Cornwall   Sweet Gonoril, I long to see thy face
           Which hast so kindly gratified my love.

Enter the King of CAMBRIA *booted and spurred, with a wand and a letter* [*and* SERVANT]

Cambria   (*looks on the letter*)
           Get a fresh horse! For, by my soul, I swear
           I am past patience longer to forbear   10
           The wished sight of my beloved mistress
           Dear Ragan, stay and comfort of my life.

Servant   (*to himself*) Now what in God's name doth my lord intend?
           He thinks he ne'er shall come at's journey's end.
           I would he had old Daedalus's waxen wings
           That he might fly – so I might stay behind.
           For e'er we get to Troynovant, I see,
           He quite will tire himself, his horse and me.

CORNWALL *and* CAMBRIA *look one upon another, and start to see each
                                                                   other there*

Cornwall   Brother of Cambria, we greet you well

	As one whom here we little did expect. 20

Cambria   Brother of Cornwall, met in happy time!
I thought as much to have met with the Sultan of Persia
As to have met you in this place, my lord.
No doubt it is about some great affairs
That makes you here so slenderly accompanied?

Cornwall   To say the truth, my lord, it is no less.
And, for your part, some hasty wind of chance
Hath blown you hither thus upon the sudden?

Cambria   My lord, to break off further circumstances –
For at this time I cannot brook delays –   30
Tell you your reason, I will tell you mine.

Cornwall   In faith, content; and therefore, to be brief –
For I am sure my haste's as great as yours –
I am sent for to come unto King Leir
Who, by these present letters [*shows letters*], promiseth
His eldest daughter, lovely Gonoril,
To me in marriage, and for present dowry
The moiety of half his regiment.
The lady's love I long ago possessed,
But until now I never had the father's.   40

Cambria   You tell me wonders! Yet I will relate
Strange news, and henceforth we must brothers call.
Witness these lines [*shows letters*]: his honourable age,
Being weary of the troubles of his crown,
His princely daughter Ragan will bestow
On me in marriage, with half his seigneuries –
Whom I would gladly have accepted of
With the third part, her complements are such.

Cornwall   If I have one half, and you have the other,

	Then between us we must needs have the whole. 50
Cambria	The hole! How mean you that? 'Sblood! I hope ⌉ ₍ₒₗ
	We shall have two holes between us. ⌋
Cornwall	Why, the whole kingdom.
Cambria	Ay, that's very true.
Cordella	What then is left for his third daughter's dowry,
	Lovely Cordella, whom the world admires?
Cambria	'Tis very strange. I know not what to think,
	Unless they mean to make a nun of her.
Cornwall	'Twere pity such rare beauty should be hid
	Within the compass of a cloister's wall; 60
	But, howsoe'er, if Leir's words prove true,
	It will be good, my lord, for me and you.
Cambria	Then let us haste all danger to prevent,
	For fear delays do alter his intent. *Exeunt*

[2.3]

Enter GONORIL *and* RAGAN

Gonoril	Sister, when did you see Cordella last,
	That pretty piece that thinks none good enough
	To speak to her because, sir-reverence,
	She hath a little beauty extraordinary?
Ragan	Since time my father warn'd her from his presence,
	I never saw her that I can remember.
	God give her joy of her surpassing beauty;
	I think her dowry will be small enough.
Gonoril	I have incens'd my father so against her
	As he will never be reclaim'd again. 10

Ragan	I was not much behind to do the like.
Gonoril	Faith, sister, what moves you to bear her such good will?
Ragan	In truth, I think the same that moveth you: Because she doth surpass us both in beauty.
Gonoril	Beshrew your fingers, how right you can guess! I tell you true, it cuts me to the heart.
Ragan	But we will keep her low enough, I warrant, And clip her wings for mounting up too high.
Gonoril	Whoever hath her shall have a rich marriage of her.
Ragan	She were right fit to make a parson's wife, 20 For they, men say, do love fair women well And many times do marry them with nothing.
Gonoril	With nothing! Marry, God forbid. Why, are there any such?
Ragan	I mean, no money.
Gonoril	I cry you mercy, I mistook you much. And she is far too stately for the church: She'll lay her husband's benefice on her back Even in one gown, if she may have her will.
Ragan	In faith, poor soul, I pity her a little. Would she were less fair or more fortunate. 30 Well, I think long until I see my Morgan, The gallant prince of Cambria, here arrive.
Gonoril	And so do I until the Cornwall king Present himself to consummate my joys. Peace, here cometh my father.

Enter LEIR, PERILLUS and [Nobles]

Leir	Cease, good my lords, and sue not to reverse Our censure which is now irrevocable.

We have dispatched letters of contract
Unto the kings of Cambria and of Cornwall;
Our hand and seal will justify no less.   40
Then do not so dishonour me, my lords,
As to make shipwreck of our kingly word.
I am as kind as is the pelican,
That kills itself to save her young ones' lives;
And yet as jealous as the princely eagle,
That kills her young ones if they do but dazzle
Upon the radiant splendour of the sun.
Within this two days I expect their coming.

Enter Kings of CORNWALL *and* CAMBRIA

But in good time they are arriv'd already.
This haste of yours, my lords, doth testify   50
The fervent love you bear unto my daughters,
And think yourselves as welcome to King Leir
As ever Priam's children were to him.

Cornwall   My gracious lord – and father too, I hope –
Pardon for that I made no greater haste;
But were my horse as swift as was my will
I long ere this had seen your majesty.

Cambria   No other 'scuse of absence can I frame
Than what my brother hath inform'd your grace;
For our undeserved welcome, we do vow   60
Perpetually to rest at your command

Cornwall   But you, sweet love, illustrious Gonoril,
The regent and the sovereign of my soul,
Is Cornwall welcome to your excellency?

Gonoril   As welcome as Leander was to Hero,
Or brave Aeneas to the Carthage queen,

So and more welcome is your grace to me.

Cambria
Oh, may my fortune prove no worse than his,
Since heav'ns do know, my fancy is as much.
Dear Ragan, say if welcome unto thee: 70
All welcomes else will little comfort me.

Ragan
As gold is welcome to the covetous eye,
As sleep is welcome to the traveller,
As is fresh water to sea-beaten men,
Or moisten'd showers unto the parched ground,
Or anything more welcomer than this,
So and more welcome lovely Morgan is.

Leir
What resteth then but that we consummate
The celebration of these nuptial rites?
My kingdom I do equally divide.   80
Princes, draw lots, and take your chance as falls.

                [CAMBRIA and CORNWALL] draw lots

These I resign as freely unto you
As erst by true succession they were mine.
And here I do freely dispossess myself
And make you two my true-adopted heirs.
Myself will sojourn with my son of Cornwall
And take me to my prayers and my beads.
I know my daughter Ragan will be sorry
Because I do not spend my days with her.
Would I were able to be with both at once;   90
They are the kindest girls in Christendom!

Perillus
I have been silent all this while, my lord,
To see if any worthier than myself
Would once have spoke in poor Cordella's cause,
But love or fear ties silence to their tongues.

<table>
<tr><td></td><td>Oh, hear me speak for her, my gracious lord,
Whose deeds have not deserv'd this ruthless doom
As thus to disinherit her of all.</td><td></td></tr>
<tr><td>Leir</td><td>Urge this no more, an if thou love thy life!
I say she is no daughter that doth scorn
To tell her father how she loveth him.
Whoever speaketh hereof to me again
I will esteem him for my mortal foe.
Come, let us in, to celebrate with joy
The happy nuptials of these lovely pairs.</td><td>100</td></tr>
</table>

Exeunt [all but] PERILLUS

Perillus	Ah, who so blind as they that will not see The near approach of their own misery? Poor lady, I extremely pity her, And, whilst I live, each drop of my heart-blood Will I strain forth to do her any good.	109 *Exit*

[2.4]

    Enter the King of GALLIA, *and* MUMFORD, *disguised like pilgrims*

Mumford	My lord, how do you brook this British air?
Gallia	'My lord'? I told you of this foolish humour And bound you to the contrary, you know.
Mumford	Pardon me for once, my lord; I did forget.
Gallia	'My lord' again? Then let's have nothing else And so be ta'en for spies, and then 'tis well.
Mumford	Zounds, I could bite my tongue in two for anger! For God's sake, name yourself some proper name.
Gallia	Call me Tresillus; I'll call thee Denapoll.

Mumford	Might I be made the monarch of the world, 10
	I could not hit upon these names, I swear.
Gallia	Then call me Will; I'll call thee Jack.
Mumford	Well, be it so, for I have well deserv'd to be call'd Jack.
Gallia	Stand close, for here a British lady cometh.

Enter CORDELLA

A fairer creature ne'er mine eyes beheld.

Cordella	[*to herself*] This is a day of joy unto my sisters
	Wherein they both are married unto kings;
	And I, by birth as worthy as themselves,
	Am turn'd into the world to seek my fortune.
	How may I blame the fickle queen of chance 20
	That maketh me a pattern of her power?
	Ah, poor weak maid, whose imbecility
	Is far unable to endure these brunts!
	Oh, father Leir, how dost thou wrong thy child
	Who always was obedient to thy will!
	But why accuse I Fortune and my father?
	No, no, it is the pleasure of my God,
	And I do willingly embrace the rod.
Gallia	It is no Goddess, for she doth complain
	On Fortune and th'unkindness of her father. 30
Cordella	These costly robes, ill-fitting my estate,
	I will exchange for other, meaner habit.
Mumford	Now if I had a kingdom in my hands
	I would exchange it for a milkmaid's smock and petticoat,
	That she and I might shift our clothes together.
Cordella	I will betake me to my thread and needle

	And earn my living with my fingers' ends.	
Mumford	Oh brave! God willing, thou shalt have my custom – By sweet Saint Denis, here I sadly swear – For all the shirts and nightgear that I wear.	40
Cordella	I will profess and vow a maiden's life.	
Mumford	Then I protest thou shalt not have my custom.	
Gallia	I can forbear no longer for to speak, For, if I do, I think my heart will break.	
Mumford	'Sblood, Will, I hope you are not in love with my seamster.	
Gallia	I am in such a labyrinth of love As that I know not which way to get out.	
Mumford	You'll ne'er get out, unless you first get in.	
Gallia	I prithee, Jack, cross not my passions!	
Mumford	Prithee, Will, to her and try her patience.	50
Gallia	Thou fairest creature, whatsoe'er thou art, That ever any mortal eyes beheld, Vouchsafe to me, who have o'erheard thy woes, To show the cause of these thy sad laments.	
Cordella	Ah, pilgrims, what avails to show the cause When there's no means to find a remedy?	
Gallia	To utter grief doth ease a heart o'ercharg'd.	
Cordella	To touch a sore doth aggravate the pain.	
Gallia	The silly mouse, by virtue of her teeth, Releas'd the princely lion from the net.	60
Cordella	Kind palmer, which so much desir'st to hear The tragic tale of my unhappy youth, Know this in brief: I am the hapless daughter	

Of Leir, sometime king of Brittany.

Gallia Why, who debars his honourable age
From being still the king of Brittany?

Cordella None but himself hath dispossess'd himself,
And given all his kingdom to the kings
Of Cornwall and of Cambria with my sisters.

Gallia Hath he giv'n nothing to your lovely self? 70

Cordella He lov'd me not, and therefore gave me nothing,
Only because I could not flatter him;
And in this day of triumph to my sisters
Doth Fortune triumph in my overthrow.

Gallia Sweet lady, say there should come a king
As good as either of your sisters' husbands
To crave your love. Would you accept of him?

Cordella Oh, do not mock with those in misery,
Nor do not think, though Fortune have the power
To spoil mine honour and debase my state, 80
That she hath any interest in my mind.
For if the greatest monarch on the earth
Should sue to me in this extremity,
Except my heart could love and heart could like
Better than any that I ever saw,
His great estate no more should move my mind
Than mountains move by blast of every wind.

Gallia Think not, sweet nymph, 'tis holy palmers' guise
To grieved souls fresh torments to devise;
Therefore, in witness of my true intent, 90
Let heav'n and earth bear record of my words:
There is a young and lusty Gallian king,
So like to me as I am to myself,

	That earnestly doth crave to have thy love And join with thee in Hymen's sacred bonds.	
Cordella	[aside] The like to thee did ne'er these eyes behold. Oh, live to add new torments to my grief! Why didst thou thus entrap me unawares? Ah, palmer, my estate doth not befit A kingly marriage as the case now stands. Whilom, whenas I liv'd in honour's height, A prince perhaps might postulate my love; Now misery, dishonour and disgrace Hath light on me and quite revers'd the case. Thy king will hold thee wise if thou surcease The suit whereas no dowry will ensue. Then be advised, palmer, what to do; Cease for thy king, seek for thyself to woo.	100
Gallia	Your birth's too high for any but a king.	
Cordella	My mind is low enough to love a palmer Rather than any king upon the earth.	110
Gallia	Oh, but you never can endure their life Which is so straight and full of penury.	
Cordella	Oh yes, I can, and happy if I might. I'll hold thy palmer's staff within my hand And think it is the sceptre of a queen. Sometime I'll set thy bonnet on my head And think I wear a rich imperial crown. Sometime I'll help thee in thy holy prayers And think I am with thee in paradise. Thus I'll mock Fortune as she mocketh me And never will my lovely choice repent, For having thee, I shall have all content.	120

Gallia	'Twere sin to hold her longer in suspense,
	Since that my soul hath vow'd she shall be mine.
	Ah, dear Cordella, cordial to my heart,
	I am no palmer as I seem to be
	But hither come, in this unknown disguise,
	To view th'admired beauty of those eyes.
	I am the king of Gallia, gentle maid, 130
	Although thus slenderly accompanied,
	And yet thy vassal by imperious love,
	And sworn to serve thee everlastingly.
Cordella	Whate'er you be, of high or low descent,
	All's one to me. I do request but this:
	That as I am, you will accept of me –
	And I will have you whatsoe'er you be.
	Yet well I know you come of royal race
	I see such sparks of honour in your face.
Mumford	Have palmers' weeds such power to win fair ladies? 140
	Faith, then I hope the next that falls is mine.
	Upon condition I no worse might speed,
	I would forever wear a palmer's weed.
	I like an honest and plain-dealing wench
	That swears without exceptions 'I will have you'.
	These foppets, that know not whether to love a man
	or no except they first go ask their mother's leave –
	by this hand, I hate them ten times worse than poison.
Gallia	What resteth then our happiness to procure?
Mumford	Faith, go to church to make the matter sure. 150
Gallia	It shall be so, because the world shall say
	King Leir's three daughters were wedded in one day.
	The celebration of this happy chance

We will defer until we come to France.

Mumford   I like the wooing that's not long a doing.
Well, for her sake, I know what I know: I'll never marry
whilst I live, except I have one of these British ladies – my
humour is alienated from the maids of France.   *Exeunt*

[3.1]

Enter PERILLUS [*alone*]

Perillus   The king hath dispossess'd himself of all,
Those to advance which scarce will give him thanks.
His youngest daughter he hath turn'd away
And no man knows what is become of her.
He sojourns now in Cornwall with the eldest,
Who flatter'd him until she did obtain
That at his hands which now she doth possess;
And now she sees he hath no more to give,
It grieves her heart to see her father live.
Oh, whom should man trust in this wicked age   10
When children thus against their parents rage?
But he, the mirror of mild patience,
Puts up all wrongs and never gives reply;
Yet shames she not, in most opprobrious sort,
To call him 'fool' and 'dotard' to his face,
And sets her parasites, of purpose, oft
In scoffing wise to offer him disgrace.
O iron age! O times! O monstrous, vild,
When parents are contemned of the child!
His pension she hath half restrain'd from him,   20
And will, e'er long, the other half, I fear,
For she thinks nothing is bestow'd in vain
But that which doth her father's life maintain.
Trust not alliance, but trust strangers rather,
Since daughters prove disloyal to the father.
Well, I will counsel him the best I can.
Would I were able to redress his wrong!
Yet what I can, unto my utmost power,
He shall be sure of to the latest hour.   *Exit*

[3.2]

Enter GONORIL, *and* SCALIGER

Gonoril
I prithee, Scaliger, tell me what thou think'st.
Could any woman of our dignity
Endure such quips and peremptory taunts
As I do daily from my doting father?
Doth't not suffice that I him keep of alms,
Who is not able for to keep himself,
But, as if he were our better, he should think
To check and snap me up at every word?
I cannot make me a new-fashion'd gown,
And set it forth with more than common cost,   10
But his old doting doltish withered wit
Is sure to give a senseless check for it.
I cannot make a banquet extraordinary
To grace myself and spread my name abroad,
But he, old fool, is captious by and by,
And saith the cost would well suffice for twice.
Judge then, I pray, what reason is't that I
Should stand alone charg'd with his vain expense
And that my sister Ragan should go free,
To whom he gave as much as unto me?   20
I prithee, Scaliger, tell me if thou know
By any means to rid me of this woe.

Scaliger
Your many favours still bestowed on me
Bind me in duty to advise your grace
How you may soonest remedy this ill.
The large allowance which he hath from you
Is that which makes him so forget himself;
Therefore abridge it half and you shall see
That having less he will more thankful be.
For why? Abundance maketh us forget   30

The fountains whence the benefits do spring.

Gonoril	Well, Scaliger, for thy kind advice herein

Gonoril   Well, Scaliger, for thy kind advice herein
I will not be ungrateful, if I live.
I have restrained half his portion already,
And I will presently restrain the other
That, having no means to relieve himself,
He may go seek elsewhere for better help.   *Exit*

Scaliger   Go, viperous woman, shame to all thy sex!
The heav'ns, no doubt, will punish thee for this
And me – a villain that, to curry favour,   40
Have given the daughter counsel 'gainst the father.
But us the world doth this experience give:
That he that cannot flatter cannot live.   *Exit*

[3.3]
     Enter King of CORNWALL, LEIR, PERILLUS *and Nobles*

Cornwall   Father, what aileth you to be so sad?
Methinks you frolic not as you were wont.

Leir   The nearer we do grow unto our graves,
The less we do delight in worldly joys.

Cornwall   But if a man can frame himself to mirth,
It is a mean for to prolong his life.

Leir   Then welcome sorrow, Leir's only friend,
Who doth desire his troubled days had end.

Cornwall   Comfort yourself, father. Here comes your daughter,
Who much will grieve, I know, to see you sad.   10

Leir   [*aside*] But more doth grieve, I fear, to see me live.

     Enter GONORIL

Cornwall	My Gonoril, you come in wished time To put your father from these pensive dumps. In faith, I fear that all things go not well.
Gonoril	What, do you fear that I have angered him? Hath he complain'd of me unto my lord? I'll provide him a piece of bread and cheese, For in a time he'll practise nothing else Than carry tales from one unto another; 'Tis all his practise for to kindle strife 20 'Twixt you, my lord, and me, your loving wife. But I will take an order, if I can, To cease th'effect where first the cause began.
Cornwall	Sweet, be not angry in a partial cause: He ne'er complained of thee in all his life. Father, you must not weigh a woman's words!
Leir	Alas, not I; poor soul, she breeds young bones And that is it makes her so touchy, sure.
Gonoril	What, breeds young bones already! You will make An honest woman of me then, belike. 30 Oh, vile old wretch – whoever heard the like? That seeketh thus his own child to defame!
Cornwall	I cannot stay to hear this discord sound. *Exit*
Gonoril	For anyone that loves your company You may go pack, and seek some other place To sow the seed of discord and disgrace. *Exit*
Leir	Thus say or do the best that e'er I can, 'Tis wrested straight into another sense. This punishment my heavy sins deserve, And more than this ten thousand thousand times, 40 Else aged Leir them could never find

	Cruel to him to whom he hath been kind.	
	Why do I overlive myself to see	
	The course of nature quite revers'd in me?	
	Ah, gentle Death, if ever any wight	
	Did wish thy presence with a perfect zeal,	
	Then come, I pray thee, even with all my heart,	
	And end my sorrows with thy fatal dart. (*Weeps*)	
Perillus	Ah, do not so disconsolate yourself,	
	Nor dew your aged cheeks with wasting tears.	50
Leir	What man art thou that takest any pity	
	Upon the worthless state of old Leir?	
Perillus	One who doth bear as great a share of grief	
	As if it were my dearest father's case.	
Leir	Ah, good my friend, how ill art thou advis'd	
	For to consort with miserable men.	
	Go learn to flatter where thou mayst in time,	
	Get favour 'mongst the mighty, and so climb;	
	For now I am so poor and full of want	
	As that I ne'er can recompense thy love.	60
Perillus	What's got by flattery doth not long endure,	
	And men in favour live not most secure.	
	My conscience tells me, if I should forsake you	
	I were the hateful'st excrement on the earth,	
	Which well do know, in course of former time,	
	How good my lord hath been to me and mine.	
Leir	Did I e'er raise thee higher than the rest	
	Of all thy ancestors which were before?	
Perillus	I ne'er did seek it, but by your good grace	
	I still enjoy'd my own with quietness.	70
Leir	Did I e'er give thee living to increase	

	The due revenues which thy father left?
Perillus	I had enough, my lord and, having that,
	What should you need to give me any more?
Leir	Oh, did I ever dispossess myself
	And give thee half my kingdom in good will?
Perillus	Alas, my lord, there were no reason why
	You should have such a thought to give it me.

Leir Nay, if thou talk of reason, then be mute,
For with good reason I can thee confute: 80
If they, which first by nature's sacred law
Do owe to me the tribute of their lives,
If they to whom I always have been kind
And bountiful beyond comparison,
If they for whom I have undone myself
And brought my age unto this extreme want,
Do now reject, contemn, despise, abhor me,
What reason moveth thee to sorrow for me?

Perillus Where reason fails, let tears confirm my love
And speak how much your passions do me move.   90
Ah, good my lord, condemn not all for one:
You have two daughters left to whom, I know,
You shall be welcome if you please to go.

Leir Oh, how thy words add sorrow to my soul
To think of my unkindness to Cordella
Whom, causeless, I did dispossess of all,
Upon th'unkind suggestions of her sisters.
And for her sake, I think, this heavy doom
Is fall'n on me, and not without desert.
Yet unto Ragan was I always kind   100
And gave to her the half of all I had;

It may be, if I should to her repair,
She would be kinder and entreat me fair.

Perillus No doubt she would, and practise, ere't be long,
By force of arms for to redress your wrong.

Leir Well, since thou dost advise me for to go,
I am resolv'd to try the worst of woe.   *Exeunt*

[3.4]

Enter RAGAN [*alone*]

Ragan How may I bless the hour of my nativity
Which bodeth unto me such happy stars!
How may I thank kind Fortune, that vouchsafes
To all my actions such desir'd event!
I rule the king of Cambria as I please;
The states are all obedient to my will;
And look what e'er I say, it shall be so;
Not anyone that dareth answer no.
My eldest sister lives in royal state
And wanteth nothing fitting her degree,   10
Yet hath she such a cooling card withal
As that her honey savoureth much of gall.
My father with her is quartermaster still
And many times restrains her of her will –
But if he were with me and serv'd me so
I'd send him packing somewhere else to go;
I'd entertain him with such slender cost
That he should quickly wish to change his host.   *Exit*

[3.5]

Enter CORNWALL, GONORIL [*with a purse and letters*]*, and*

Attendants

Cornwall	Ah, Gonoril, what dire unhappy chance
	Hath sequester'd thy father from our presence
	That no report can yet be heard of him?
	Some great unkindness hath been offer'd him
	Exceeding far the bounds of patience,
	Else all the world shall never me persuade
	He would forsake us without notice made.

Gonoril Alas, my lord, whom doth it touch so near,
Or who hath interest in this grief but I,
Whom sorrow had brought to her longest home,   10
But that I know his qualities so well?
I know he is but stol'n upon my sister
At unawares to see her how she fares,
And spend a little time with her to note
How all things go and how she likes her choice,
And when occasion serves, he'll steal from her
And unawares return to us again.
Therefore, my lord, be frolic, and resolve
To see my father here again ere long.

Cornwall I hope so too, but yet, to be more sure,   20
I'll send a post immediately to know
Whether he be arrived there or no.   *Exit*

Gonoril [*aside*] But I will intercept the messenger
And temper him, before he doth depart,
With sweet persuasions and with sound rewards,
That his report shall ratify my speech
And make my lord cease further to inquire.
If he be not gone to my sister's court,
As sure my mind presageth that he is,
He haply may, by travelling unknown ways,   30

Fall sick and, as a common passenger,
Be dead and buried. Would God 'twere so well,
For then there were no more to-do but this:
He went away and none knows where he is.
But say he be in Cambria with the king
And there exclaim against me as he will,
I know he is as welcome to my sister
As water is into a broken ship.
Well, after him I'll send such thunderclaps
Of slander, scandal and invented tales   40
That all the blame shall be remov'd from me
And unperceiv'd rebound upon himself.
Thus with one nail another I'll expel
And make the world judge that I us'd him well.

Enter the MESSENGER *that should go to Cambria, with letter[s] in his hand*

Gonoril	My honest friend, whither away so fast?
Messenger	To Cambria, madam, with letters from the king.
Gonoril	To whom?
Messenger	Unto your father, if he be there.
Gonoril	Let me see them. (*Opens them*)
Messenger	Madam, I hope your grace will stand between me 50 and my neck-verse if I be called in question for opening the king's letters.
Gonoril	'Twas I that opened them; it was not thou.
Messenger	Ay, but you need not care; and so must I, a handsome man, be quickly truss'd up – and when a man's hang'd, all the world cannot save him.
Gonoril	He that hangs thee were better hang his father,

Or that but hurts thee in the least degree:
I tell thee, we make great account of thee.

Messenger I am o'er-joy'd, I surfeit of sweet words. Kind   60
queen, had I a hundred lives I would spend ninety-
nine of them for you for that word.

Gonoril Ay, but thou wouldst keep one life still –
And that's as many as thou art like to have.

Messenger That one life is not too dear for my good queen.
This sword, this buckler, this head, this heart, these
hands, arms, legs, tripes, bowels and all the members
else whatsoever are at your dispose: use me, trust
me, command me. If I fail in anything, tie me to a
dung-cart and make a scavenger's horse of me, and   70
whip me so long as I have any skin on my back.

Gonoril In token of further employment, take that. (*Flings him a purse*)

Messenger A strong bond, a firm obligation, good in law, good
in law. If I keep not the condition, let my neck be
the forfeiture of my negligence.

Gonoril I like thee well; thou hast a good tongue.

Messenger And as bad a tongue, if it be set on it, as any oyster-
wife at Billingsgate hath! Why, I have made many
of my neighbours forsake their houses, with
railing upon them, and go dwell elsewhere; and so   80
by my means houses have been good cheap in our
parish. My tongue, being well whetted with choler,
is more sharp than a razor of Palermo.

Gonoril Oh, thou art a fit man for my purpose.

Messenger Commend me not, sweet queen, before you try me;
As my deserts are, so do think of me.

Gonoril	Well said! Then this is thy trial: instead of carrying the king's letters to my father, carry thou these letters to my sister [*gives him letters*], which contain matter quite contrary to the other. There 90 shall she be given to understand that my father hath detracted her, given out slanderous speeches against her, and that he hath most intolerably abused me, set my lord and me at variance and made mutinies amongst the commons. These things, although it be not so, Yet thou must affirm them to be true With oaths and protestations as will serve To drive my sister out of love with him And cause my will accomplished to be. 100 This do, thou win'st my favour forever, and makest a highway of preferment to thee and all thy friends.
Messenger	It sufficeth: conceit it is already done. I will so tongue-whip him, that I will leave him as bare of credit as a poulter leaves a cony when she pulls off his skin.
Gonoril	Yet there is a further matter.
Messenger	I thirst to hear it.
Gonoril	If my sister thinketh convenient, as my letters importeth, to make him away, hast thou the heart 110 to effect it?
Messenger	Few words are best in so small a matter; these are but trifles. By this book I will! (*Kiss*[*es*] *the paper*)
Gonoril	About it presently. I long till it be done.
Messenger	I fly, I fly. *Exeunt*

[4.1]

Enter CORDELLA [*alone*]

Cordella   I have been over-negligent today
In going to the temple of my God
To render thanks for all His benefits
Which He miraculously hath bestow'd on me
In raising me out of my mean estate
Whenas I was devoid of worldly friends
And placing me in such a sweet content
As far exceeds the reach of my deserts.
My kingly husband, mirror of his time
For zeal, for justice, kindness and for care   10
To God, his subjects, me and common weal,
By His appointment was ordain'd for me.
I cannot wish the thing that I do want;
I cannot want the thing but I may have –
Save only this which I shall ne'er obtain:
My father's love. Oh, this I ne'er shall gain.
I would abstain from any nutriment
And pine my body to the very bones;
Barefoot I would on pilgrimage set forth
Unto the furthest quarters of the earth,   20
And all my lifetime would I sackcloth wear
And mourning-wise pour dust upon my head,
So he but to forgive me once would please,
That his grey hairs might go to heav'n in peace.
And yet I know not how I him offended,
Or wherein justly I have deserved blame.
O sisters! You are much to blame in this:
It was not he, but you that did me wrong!
Yet God forgive both him and you and me,
E'en as I do in perfect charity.   30

I will to church and pray unto my Saviour
That, e'er I die, I may obtain his favour.   *Exit*

[4.2]
                         Enter LEIR *and* PERILLUS *faintly*

Perillus   Rest on me, my lord, and stay yourself:
             The way seems tedious to your aged limbs.

Leir   Nay, rest on me, kind friend, and stay thyself:
             Thou art as old as I, but more kind.

Perillus   Ah, good my lord, it ill befits that I
             Should lean upon the person of a king.

Leir   But it fits worse that I should bring thee forth,
             That had no cause to come along with me
             Through these uncouth paths and tireful ways
             And never ease thy fainting limbs a whit.   10
             Thou hast left all – ay, all – to come with me,
             And I, for all, have nought to guerdon thee.

Perillus   Cease, good my lord, to aggravate my woes
             With these kind words which cuts my heart in two
             To think your will should want the pow'r to do.

Leir   Cease, good Perillus, for to call me lord,
             And think me but the shadow of myself.

Perillus   That honourable title will I give
             Unto my lord so long as I do live.
             Oh, be of comfort, for I see the place   20
             Whereas your daughter keeps her residence.
             And, lo, in happy time the Cambrian prince
             Is here arriv'd to gratify our coming.

         Enter the [king] *of* CAMBRIA, RAGAN *and Nobles*[;LEIR *and*

PERILLUS] *look upon them, and whisper together*

Leir	[*apart to* PERILLUS] Were I best speak, or sit me down and die? I am asham'd to tell this heavy tale.
Perillus	[*apart to* LEIR] Then let me tell it, if you please, my lord: 'Tis shame for them that were the cause thereof.
Cambria	What two old men are those that seem so sad? Methinks I should remember well their looks.
Ragan	No, I mistake not! Sure it is my father! 30 [*Aside*] I must dissemble kindness now of force – (*run*[*s*] *to him, and kneels down*) Father, I bid you welcome, full of grief To see your grace us'd thus unworthily And ill-befitting for your reverend age. To come on foot a journey so endurable! Oh, what disaster chance hath been the cause To make your cheeks so hollow, spare and lean? He cannot speak for weeping. For God's love, come! Let us refresh him with some needful things, And, at more leisure, we may better know 40 Whence springs the ground of this unlook'd-for woe.
Cambria	Come, father! Ere we any further talk You shall refresh you after this weary walk. *Exeunt* [*all but*] RAGAN
Ragan	Comes he to me with finger in the eye To tell a tale against my sister here, Whom I do know he greatly hath abus'd? And now, like a contentious crafty wretch, He first begins for to complain himself,

Whenas himself is in the greatest fault.
I'll not be partial in my sister's cause,   50
Nor yet believe his doting vain reports,
Who, for a trifle, safely I dare say,
Upon a spleen is stolen thence away,
And here, forsooth, he hopeth to have harbour,
And to be moan'd and made on like a child.
But ere't be long, his coming he shall curse,
And truly say he came from bad to worse.
Yet will I make fair weather, to procure
Convenient means, and then I'll strike it sure.   *Exit*

[4.3]

Enter MESSENGER [*alone, holding letters*]

Messenger   Now happily I am arrived here
Before the stately palace of the Cambrian king.
If Leir be here safe-seated and in rest,
To rouse him from it I will do my best.

Enter RAGAN [*with a purse*]

Now, bags of gold, your virtue is, no doubt,
To make me in my message bold and stout.
[*To* RAGAN] The King of Heaven preserve your majesty
And send your highness everlasting reign!

Ragan   Thanks, good my friend; but what imports thy message?

Messenger   Kind greetings from the Cornwall queen;   10
The residue these letters will declare.

Ragan   (*opens the letters*) How fares our royal sister?

Messenger   I did leave her at my parting in good health.

[RAGAN] *reads the letter*[*s*]*, frowns and stamps*

[*Aside*] See how her colour comes and goes again,
Now red as scarlet, now as pale as ash;
See how she knits her brow and bites her lips
And stamps and makes a dumb-show of disdain
Mix'd with revenge and violent extremes.
Here will be more work and more crowns for me.

Ragan   [*aside*] Alas, poor soul, and hath he us'd her thus?   20
And is he now come hither with intent
To set divorce betwixt my lord and me?
Doth he give out that he doth hear report
That I do rule my husband as I list,
And therefore means to alter so the case
That I shall know my lord to be my head?
Well, it were best for him to take good heed,
Or I will make him hop without a head
For his presumption, dotard that he is!
In Cornwall he hath made such mutinies –   30
First, setting of the king against the queen,
Then stirring up the commons 'gainst the king –
That had he there continu'd any longer,
He had been call'd in question for his fact.
So, upon that occasion, thence he fled
And comes thus slyly stealing unto us.
And now, already, since his coming hither,
My lord and he are grown in such a league
That I can have no conference with his grace.
I fear he doth already intimate   40
Some forged cavillations 'gainst my state.
'Tis therefore best to cut him off in time,
Lest slanderous rumours once abroad dispers'd
It is too late for them to be revers'd –
[*to* MESSENGER] Friend, as the tenor of these letters
                       shows,

	My sister puts great confidence in thee.	
Messenger	She never yet committed trust to me	
	But that, I hope, she found me always faithful.	
	So will I be to any friend of hers	
	That hath occasion to employ my help.	50
Ragan	Hast thou the heart to act a stratagem,	
	And give a stab or two if need require?	
Messenger	I have a heart compact of adamant,	
	Which never knew what melting pity meant.	
	I weigh no more the murd'ring of a man	
	Than I respect the cracking of a flea	
	When I do catch her biting on my skin.	
	If you will have your husband or your father	
	Or both of them sent to another world,	
	Do but command me do't; it shall be done.	60
Ragan	It is enough; we make no doubt of thee.	
	Meet us tomorrow here at nine o'clock;	
	Meanwhile, farewell, and [*gives him purse*]	
	drink that for my sake.	*Exit*
Messenger	Ay, this is it will make me do the deed.	
	Oh, had I every day such customers,	
	This were the gainful'st trade in Christendom!	
	A purse of gold giv'n for a paltry stab!	
	Why, here's a wench that longs to have a stab.	
	Well, I could give it her and ne'er hurt her neither.	[*Exit*]

[4.4]

Enter the King of GALLIA *and* CORDELLA

Gallia	When will these clouds of sorrow once disperse
	And smiling joy triumph upon thy brow?

When will this scene of sadness have an end
And pleasant acts ensue to move delight?
When will my lovely queen cease to lament
And take some comfort to her grieved thoughts?
If of thyself thou deign'st to have no care,
Yet pity me whom thy grief makes despair.

Cordella   Oh, grieve not you, my lord; you have no cause.
Let not my passions move your mind a whit,   10
For I am bound by nature to lament
For his ill will that life to me first lent.
If so the stock be dried with disdain,
Wither'd and sere the branch must needs remain.

Gallia   But thou art now graft in another stock:
I am the stock, and thou the lovely branch,
And from my root continual sap shall flow
To make thee flourish with perpetual spring.
Forget thy father and thy kindred now,
Since they forsake thee like inhuman beasts.   20
Think they are dead, since all their kindness dies,
And bury them where black oblivion lies.
Think not thou art the daughter of old Leir,
Who did unkindly disinherit thee,
But think thou art the noble Gallian queen
And wife to him that dearly loveth thee.
Embrace the joys that present with thee dwell;
Let sorrow pack and hide herself in hell.

Cordella   Not that I miss my country or my kin,
My old acquaintance or my ancient friends   30
Doth any whit distemperate my mind,
Knowing you, which are more dear to me
Than country, kin and all things else can be;
Yet, pardon me, my gracious lord, in this,

For what can stop the course of nature's power?
As easy is it for four-footed beasts
To stay themselves upon the liquid air
And mount aloft into the element
And overstrip the feather'd fowls in flight;
As easy is it for the slimy fish   40
To live and thrive without the help of water;
As easy is it for the blackamoor
To wash the tawny colour from his skin,
Which all oppose against the course of nature,
As I am able to forget my father.

Gallia   Mirror of virtue, phoenix of our age,
Too kind a daughter for an unkind father,
Be of good comfort! For I will dispatch
Ambassadors immediately for Britain
Unto the king of Cornwall's court, whereas   50
Your father keepeth now his residence,
And in the kindest manner him entreat
That, setting former grievances apart,
He will be pleas'd to come and visit us.
If no entreaty will suffice the turn,
I'll offer him the half of all my crown;
If that moves not, we'll furnish out a fleet
And sail to Cornwall for to visit him,
And there you shall be firmly reconcil'd
In perfect love, as erst you were before.   60

Cordella   Where tongue cannot sufficient thanks afford,
The King of Heaven remunerate my lord.

Gallia   Only be blithe and frolic, sweet, with me,
This and much more I'll do to comfort thee.   [*Exeunt*]

[4.5]

Enter MESSENGER [*alone*]

Messenger   It is a world to see, now I am flush,
             How many friends I purchase everywhere!
             How many seeks to creep into my favour,
             And kiss their hands, and bend their knees to me!
             No more; here comes the queen. Now shall I know her mind
             And hope for to derive more crowns from her.

Enter RAGAN [*with two purses*]

Ragan   My friend, I see thou mind'st thy promise well,
             And art before me here, methinks, today.

Messenger   I am a poor man, an it like your grace,
             But yet I always love to keep my word.   10

Ragan   Well, keep thy word with me, and thou shalt see
             That of a poor man I will make thee rich.

Messenger   I long to hear it! It might have been dispatch'd
             If you had told me of it yesternight.

Ragan   It is a thing of right strange consequence,
             And well I cannot utter it in words.

Messenger   It is more strange that I am not by this
             Beside myself with longing for to hear it.
             Were it to meet the devil in his den
             And try a bout with him for a scratch'd face,   20
             I'd undertake it, if you would but bid me.

Ragan   Ah, good my friend, that I should have thee do
             Is such a thing as I do shame to speak;
             Yet it must needs be done.

Messenger   I'll speak it for thee, queen. Shall I kill thy father?

	I know 'tis that, and if it be so, say.	
Ragan	Ay.	
Messenger	Why, that's enough.	
Ragan	And yet that is not all.	
Messenger	What else?	30
Ragan	Thou must kill that old man that came with him.	
Messenger	Here are two hands; for each of them is one.	
Ragan	And for each hand here is a recompense.	

(Give[s] him two purses)

Messenger
Oh, that I had ten hands by miracle,
I could tear ten in pieces with my teeth
So in my mouth you'ld put a purse of gold.
But in what manner must it be effected?

Ragan
Tomorrow morning, ere the break of day,
I, by a wile, will send them to the thicket
That is about some two miles from the court,   40
And promise them to meet them there myself,
Because I must have private conference
About some news I have receiv'd from Cornwall.
This is enough: I know they will not fail.
And then be ready for to play thy part,
Which done, thou mayst right easily escape,
And no man once mistrust thee for the fact.
But yet, before thou prosecute the act,
Show him the letter which my sister sent;
There let him read his own indictment first,   50
And then proceed to execution.
But see thou faint not, for they will speak fair.

Messenger	Could he speak words as pleasing as the pipe
	Of Mercury, which charm'd the hundred eyes
	Of watchful Argus and enforc'd him sleep,
	Yet here ([*gestures*] *to the purse*)
	are words so pleasing to my thoughts
	As quite shall take away the sound of his. *Exit*
Ragan	About it then, and when thou hast dispatch'd,
	I'll find a means to send thee after him. *Exit*

[4.6]

Enter CORNWALL *and* GONORIL

Cornwall	I wonder that the messenger doth stay
	Whom we dispatch'd for Cambria so long since.
	If that his answer do not please us well,
	And he do show good reason for delay,
	I'll teach him how to dally with his king
	And to detain us in such long suspense.
Gonoril	My lord, I think the reason may be this:
	My father means to come along with him,
	And therefore 'tis his pleasure he shall stay
	For to attend upon him on the way. 10
Cornwall	It may be so and, therefore, till I know
	The truth thereof, I will suspend my judgement.

Enter SERVANT

Servant	An't like your grace, there is an ambassador arrived
	from Gallia, and craves admittance to your majesty.
Cornwall	From Gallia? What should his message
	Hither import? Is not your father haply
	Gone thither? Well, whatsoe'er it be,

Bid him come in, he shall have audience.

Enter AMBASSADOR

What news from Gallia? Speak, Ambassador.

Ambassador   The noble king and queen of Gallia first salutes,   20
By me, their honourable father, my lord Leir;
Next, they commend them kindly to your graces,
As those whose welfare they entirely wish.
Letters I have to deliver to my lord Leir,
And presents too, if I might speak with him.

Gonoril   If you might speak with him? Why, do you think
We are afraid that you should speak with him?

Ambassador   Pardon me, madam, for I think not so,
But say so only 'cause he is not here.

Cornwall   Indeed, my friend, upon some urgent cause   30
He is at this time absent from the court,
But if a day or two you here repose,
'Tis very likely you shall have him here,
Or else have certain notice where he is.

Gonoril   Are not we worthy to receive your message?

Ambassador   I had in charge to do it to himself.

Gonoril   (*to herself*) It may be then 'twill not be done in haste –
How doth my sister brook the air of France?

Ambassador   Exceeding well, and never sick one hour
Since first she set her foot upon the shore.   40

Gonoril   I am the more sorry.

Ambassador   I hope not so, madam.

Gonoril   Didst thou not say that she was ever sick

	Since the first hour that she arrived there?
Ambassador	No, madam, I said quite contrary.
Gonoril	Then I mistook thee.
Cornwall	Then she is merry, if she have her health.
Ambassador	Oh no, her grief exceeds, until the time That she be reconcil'd unto her father.
Gonoril	God continue it.
Ambassador	What, Madam?
Gonoril	Why, her health.
Ambassador	Amen to that; but God release her grief, And send her father in a better mind Than to continue always so unkind.
Cornwall	I'll be a mediator in her cause And seek all means to expiate his wrath.
Ambassador	Madam, I hope your grace will do the like.
Gonoril	Should I be a mean to exasperate his wrath Against my sister whom I love so dear? No, no.
Ambassador	To expiate or mitigate his wrath, For he hath misconceiv'd without a cause.
Gonoril	Oh, ay, what else?
Ambassador	'Tis pity it should be so. Would it were otherwise!
Gonoril	It were great pity it should be otherwise.
Ambassador	Than how, madam?
Gonoril	Than that they should be reconcil'd again.
Ambassador	It shows you bear an honourable mind.

50

60

Gonoril	(*speaks to herself*) It shows thy understanding to be blind
	And that thou had'st need of an interpreter. 70
	Well, I will know thy message ere't be long
	And find a mean to cross it if I can.
Cornwall	Come in, my friend, and frolic in our court
	Till certain notice of my father come. *Exeunt*

[4.7]

Enter LEIR *and* PERILLUS [*each with a bag containing a book*]

Perillus	My lord, you are up today before your hour;
	'Tis news to you to be abroad so rathe.
Leir	'Tis news indeed. I am so extreme heavy,
	That I can scarcely keep my eyelids open.
Perillus	And so am I, but I impute the cause
	To rising sooner than we use to do.
Leir	Hither my daughter means to come disguis'd.
	I'll sit me down and read until she come.

[LEIR *and* PERILLUS *each*] *pull out a book* [*from their bags*] *and sit down*

Perillus	She'll not be long, I warrant you, my lord.
	But say a couple of these they call 'good fellows' 10
	Should step out of a hedge and set upon us,
	We were in good case for to answer them.
Leir	'Twere not for us to stand upon our hands.
Perillus	I fear we scant should stand upon our legs.
	But how should we do to defend ourselves?
Leir	E'en pray to God to bless us from their hands,
	For fervent prayer much ill hap withstands.
Perillus	I'll sit and pray with you for company,

Yet was I ne'er so heavy in my life.

[LEIR *and* PERILLUS] *fall both asleep*

Enter the MESSENGER *with* [*letters and*] *two daggers in his hands*

Messenger | Were it not a mad jest if two or three of my   20
| profession should meet me and lay me down in a
| ditch and play rob-thief with me, and perforce take
| my gold away from me, whilst I act this stratagem,
| and by this means the grey-beards should escape?
| Faith, when I were at liberty again, I would make
| no more to-do but go to the next tree and there hang
| myself. (*See*[*s*] *them and start*[*s*]) But stay! Methinks
| my youths are here already,
| And with pure zeal have pray'd themselves asleep.
| I think they know to what intent they came,
| And are provided for another world.   30
| *(Takes their books away)*
| Now could I stab them bravely while they sleep –
| And in a manner put them to no pain,
| And doing so I show'd them mighty friendship,
| For fear of death is worse than death itself –
| But that my sweet queen will'd me for to show
| This letter to them ere I did the deed.
| Mass, they begin to stir. I'll stand aside;
| So shall I come upon them unawares.

[LEIR *and* PERILLUS] *wake and rise*

Leir | I marvel that my daughter stays so long.

Perillus | I fear we did mistake the place, my lord.   40

Leir | God grant we don't miscarry in the place!
| I had a short nap, but so full of dread
| As much amazeth me to think thereof.

Perillus	Fear not, my lord, dreams are but fantasies
	And slight imaginations of the brain.
Messenger	[*aside*] Persuade him so, but I'll make him and you
	Confess that dreams do often prove too true.
Perillus	I pray, my lord, what was the effect of it?
	I may go near to guess what it portends.
Messenger	[*aside*] Leave that to me; I will expound the dream. 50
Leir	Methought my daughters, Gonoril and Ragan,
	Stood both before me – with such grim aspects,
	Each brandishing a falchion in their hands
	Ready to lop a limb off where it fell,
	And in their other hands a naked poniard
	Wherewith they stabb'd me in a hundred places
	And, to their thinking, left me there for dead –
	But then my youngest daughter, fair Cordella,
	Came with a box of balsam in her hand
	And poured it into my bleeding wounds, 60
	By whose good means I was recover'd well
	In perfect health as erst I was before.
	And with the fear of this I did awake,
	And yet, for fear, my feeble joints do quake.
Messenger	[*aside*] I'll make you quake for something presently –
	[*to* LEIR *and* PERILLUS] Stand! Stand!
	[LEIR *and* PERILLUS] *reel*
Leir	We do, my friend, although with much ado.
Messenger	Deliver! Deliver!
Perillus	Deliver us, good lord, from such as he.
Messenger	You should have pray'd before while it was time, 70
	And then perhaps you might have scap'd my hands;

But you, like faithful watchmen, fell asleep
The whilst I came and took your halberds from you.

(*Show*[*s*] *their books*)

And now you want your weapons of defence,
How have you any hope to be deliver'd?
This comes because you have no better stay
But fall asleep when you should watch and pray.

Leir   My friend, thou seem'st to be a proper man.

Messenger   'Sblood, how the old slave claws me by the elbow!
            He thinks, belike, to 'scape by scraping thus.   80

Perillus   And it may be, are in some need of money.

Messenger   That to be false; behold my evidence!   (*Shows his purses*)

Leir   If that I have will do thee any good,
            I give it thee e'en with a right good will.

                              [MESSENGER] *take*[*s the purse*]

Perillus   Here, take mine too, and wish with all my heart
            To do thee pleasure, it were twice as much.

Messenger   (*take*[*s second purse*], *and weigh*[*s*] *both in his hands*)
            I'll none of them; they are too light for me.

                                   (*Puts them in his pocket*)

Leir   Why then, farewell! An if thou have occasion
            In anything to use me to the queen,
            'Tis like enough that I can pleasure thee.   90

                         [LEIR *and* PERILLUS] *proffer to go*

Messenger   Do you hear? Do you hear, sir?
            If I had occasion to use you to the queen,
            Would you do one thing for me I should ask?

Leir   Ay, anything that lies within my power.

	Here is my hand upon it; so, farewell! (*Proffer[s] to go*)
Messenger	Hear you, sir! Hear you! Pray, a word with you.
	Methinks a comely honest ancient man
	Should not dissemble with one for a vantage.
	I know when I shall come to try this gear
	You will recant from all that you have said.

Messenger   Hear you, sir! Hear you! Pray, a word with you.
Methinks a comely honest ancient man
Should not dissemble with one for a vantage.
I know when I shall come to try this gear
You will recant from all that you have said.   100

Perillus   Mistrust not him, but try him when thou wilt.
He is her father; therefore may do much.

Messenger   I know he is, and therefore mean to try him.
You are his friend too; I must try you both.

Leir & Perillus   Prithee do; prithee do.

　　　　　　　　　　　　([LEIR *and* PERILLUS] *proffer to go out*)

Messenger   Stay, grey-beards, then, and prove men of your words.
The queen hath tied me by a solemn oath
Here in this place to see you both dispatch'd.
Now, for the safeguard of my conscience,
Do me the pleasure for to kill yourselves;   110
So shall you save me labour for to do it
And prove yourselves true old men of your words.
And here I vow, in sight of all the world,
I ne'er will trouble you, whilst I live, again.

Leir   Affright us not with terror, good my friend,
Nor strike such fear into our aged hearts;
Play not the cat which dallieth with the mouse
And on a sudden maketh her a pray.
But if thou art mark'd for the man of death
To me and to my Damon, tell me plain,   120
That we may be prepared for the stroke
And make ourselves fit for the world to come.

Messenger	I am the last of any mortal race
	That e'er your eyes are likely to behold,
	And hither sent of purpose to this place
	To give a final period to your days,
	Which are so wicked and have liv'd so long
	That your own children seek to short your life.
Leir	Camst thou from France of purpose to do this?
Messenger	From France? Zounds, do I look like a Frenchman? 130
	Sure I have not mine own face on. Somebody hath
	chang'd faces with me and I know not of it, but I
	am sure my apparel is all English! Sirrah, what
	mean'st thou to ask that question? I could spoil the
	fashion of this face for anger. A French face!
Leir	Because my daughter whom I have offended –
	And at whose hands I have deserv'd as ill
	As ever any father did of child –
	Is queen of France, not thanks at all to me
	But unto God who my injustice see; 140
	If it be so that she doth seek revenge,
	As with good reason she may justly do,
	I will most willingly resign my life:
	A sacrifice to mitigate her ire.
	I never will entreat thee to forgive,
	Because I am unworthy for to live.
	Therefore, speak soon – and I will soon make speed –
	Whether Cordella will'd thee do this deed? 149
Messenger	As I am a perfect gentleman, thou speak'st French to me!
	I never heard Cordella's name before,
	Nor never was in France in all my life.
	I never knew thou had'st a daughter there

To whom thou didst prove so unkind a churl;
But thy own tongue declares that thou hast been
A vile old wretch and full of heinous sin.

Leir   Ah, no, my friend, thou art deceived much,
For her except – whom I confess I wrong'd
Through doting frenzy and o'er-jealous love –
There lives not any under heav'n's bright eye   160
That can convict me of impiety.
And, therefore, sure thou dost mistake the mark,
For I am in true peace with all the world.

Messenger You are the fitter for the King of Heaven,
And therefore, for to rid thee of suspense,
Know thou: the queens of Cambria and Cornwall,
Thy own two daughters, Gonoril and Ragan,
Appointed me to massacre thee here.
Why wouldst thou then persuade me that thou art
In charity with all the world but now,   170
When thy own issue hold thee in such hate
That they have hired me t'abridge thy fate?
Oh, fie upon such vile dissembling breath
That would deceive even at the point of death!

Perillus   Am I awake or is it but a dream?

Messenger Fear nothing, man, thou art but in a dream,
And thou shalt never wake until doomsday;
By then, I hope, thou wilt have slept enough.

Leir   Yet, gentle friend, grant one thing ere I die.

Messenger I'll grant you anything except your lives.   180

Leir   Oh, but assure me, by some certain token,
That my two daughters hir'd thee to this deed.
If I were once resolv'd of that, then I

	Would wish no longer life but crave to die.
Messenger	That to be true, in sight of heav'n I swear.
Leir	Swear not by heav'n, for fear of punishment. The heav'ns are guiltless of such heinous acts.
Messenger	I swear by earth, the mother of us all.
Leir	Swear not by earth, for she abhors to bear Such bastards as are murderers of her sons.

190

Messenger	Why then, by hell and all the devils I swear.
Leir	Swear not by hell, for that stands gaping wide To swallow thee an if thou do this deed.

Thunder and lightning

Messenger [*aside*] I would that word were in his belly again:
It hath frighted me e'en to the very heart.
This old man is some strong magician;
His words have turn'd my mind from this exploit –
[*to* LEIR *and* PERILLUS]
Then neither heav'n, earth, nor hell be witness
But let this paper witness for them all.

(*Shows* GONORIL's *letter*)

Shall I relent or shall I prosecute?　　　　　200
Shall I resolve or were I best recant?
I will not crack my credit with two queens
To whom I have already pass'd my word.
Oh, but my conscience for this act doth tell
I get heav'n's hate, earth's scorn, and pains of hell.

[LEIR *and* PERILLUS] *bless themselves*

Perillus O just Jehovah, whose almighty power
Doth govern all things in this spacious world,
How canst Thou suffer such outrageous acts

	To be committed without just revenge?

To be committed without just revenge?
O viperous generation and accurst,   210
To seek his blood whose blood did make them first!

Leir Ah, my true friend in all extremity,
Let us submit us to the will of God.
Things past all sense let us not seek to know;
It is God's will, and therefore must be so.
[*To* MESSENGER] My friend, I am prepared for the
                                                        stroke.
Strike when thou wilt, and I forgive thee here,
E'en from the very bottom of my heart!

Messenger But I am not prepared for to strike.

Leir Farewell, Perillus, e'en the truest friend   220
That ever lived in adversity.
The latest kindness I'll request of thee
Is that thou go unto my daughter Cordella
And carry her her father's latest blessing.
Withal desire her that she will forgive me,
For I have wrong'd her without any cause.
Now, Lord, receive me; for I come to thee,
And die, I hope, in perfect charity.
Dispatch, I pray thee; I have lived too long.

Messenger Ay, but you are unwise to send an errand   230
By him that never meaneth to deliver it;
Why, he must go along with you to heaven;
It were not good you should go all alone.

Leir No doubt he shall, when by the course of nature
He must surrender up his due to death,
But that time shall not come till God permit.

Messenger Nay, presently, to bear you company.

	I have a passport for him in my pocket
	Already seal'd, and he must needs ride post.
	(*Show*[*s*] *a bag of money*)
Leir	The letter which I read imports not so; 240
	It only toucheth me; no word of him.
Messenger	Ay, but the queen commands it must be so,
	And I am paid for him as well as you.
Perillus	[*to* LEIR] I, who have borne you company in life,
	Most willingly will bear a share in death.
	[*To* MESSENGER] It skilleth not for me, my friend, a whit,
	Nor for a hundred such as thou and I.
Messenger	Marry, but it doth, sir. By your leave, your good
	days are past. Though it be no matter for you, 'tis a
	matter for me: proper men are not so rife! 250
Perillus	Oh, but beware how thou dost lay thy hand
	Upon the high anointed of the Lord;
	Oh, be advised ere thou dost begin:
	Dispatch me straight, but meddle not with him.
Leir	Friend, thy commission is to deal with me,
	And I am he that hath deserved all.
	The plot was laid to take away my life:
	And here it is. I do entreat thee take it!
	Yet for my sake, and as thou art a man,
	Spare this my friend that hither with me came. 260
	I brought him forth whereas he had not been
	But for good will to bear me company.
	He left his friends, his country and his goods,
	And came with me in most extremity.
	Oh, if he should miscarry here and die,
	Who is the cause of it, but only I?

Messenger	Why that am I; let that ne'er trouble thee.
Leir	Oh no, 'tis I. O, had I now to give thee
	The monarchy of all the spacious world
	To save his life, I would bestow it on thee. 270
	But I have nothing but these tears and prayers
	And the submission of a bended knee. (*Kneel*[*s*]
	Oh, if all this to mercy move thy mind
	Spare him; in heav'n thou shalt like mercy find.
Messenger	[*aside*] I am as hard to be moved as another, and yet
	methinks the strength of their persuasions stirs me a little.
Perillus	My friend, if fear of the almighty power
	Have power to move thee, we have said enough;
	But if thy mind be moveable with gold,
	We have not presently to give it thee. 280
	Yet to thyself thou mayst do greater good
	To keep thy hands still undefil'd from blood,
	For do but well consider with thyself,
	When thou hast finish'd this outrageous act
	What horror still will haunt thee for the deed!
	Think this again, that they which would incense
	Thee for to be the butcher of their father,
	When it is done, for fear it should be known,
	Would make a means to rid thee from the world.
	Oh, then art thou forever tied in chains 290
	Of everlasting torments to endure,
	Even in the hottest hole of grisly hell,
	Such pains as never mortal tongue can tell.

It thunders. [MESSENGER] *quakes, and lets fall the dagger next to* PERILLUS

Leir	Oh, heav'ns be thanked: he will spare my friend!
	Now, when thou wilt, come make an end of me.

	[MESSENGER] *lets fall the other dagger*
Perillus	Oh, happy sight! He means to save my lord!
	The King of Heaven continue this good mind.
Leir	Why stay'st thou to do execution?
Messenger	I am as wilful as you for your life.
	I will not do it now you do entreat me. 300
Perillus	Ah, now I see thou hast some spark of grace.
Messenger	Beshrew you for it; you have put it in me!
	The parlousest old men that e'er I heard!
	Well, to be flat, I'll not meddle with you.
	Here I found you, and here I'll leave you.
	If any ask you why the case so stands,
	Say that your tongues were better than your hands. *Exit*
Perillus	[*to* MESSENGER] Farewell. If ever we together meet,
	It shall go hard but I will thee re-greet.
	[To LEIR] Courage, my lord, the worst is overpast; 310
	Let us give thanks to God, and hie us hence.
Leir	[*rises*] Thou art deceiv'd, for I am past the best
	And know not whither for to go from hence.
	Death had been better welcome unto me
	Than longer life to add more misery.
Perillus	It were not good to return from whence we came,
	Unto your daughter Ragan back again.
	Now let us go to France unto Cordella,
	Your youngest daughter; doubtless she will succour you.
Leir	Oh, how can I persuade myself of that, 320
	Since th'other two are quite devoid of love
	To whom I was so kind as that my gifts
	Might make them love me, if 'twere nothing else?

Perillus	No worldly gifts, but grace from God on high
	Doth nourish virtue and true charity.
	Remember well what words Cordella spake
	What time you ask'd her how she lov'd your grace.
	She said her love unto you was as much
	As ought a child to bear unto her father.
Leir	But she did find my love was not to her 330
	As should a father bear unto a child.
Perillus	That makes not her love to be any less,
	If she do love you as a child should do.
	You have tried two; try one more for my sake.
	I'll ne'er entreat you further trial make.
	Remember well the dream you had of late
	And think what comfort it foretells to us.
Leir	Come, truest friend that ever man possess'd;
	I know thou counsel'st all things for the best.
	If this third daughter play a kinder part, 340
	It comes of God and not of my desert. *Exeunt*

[4.8]

Enter the Gallian AMBASSADOR [*alone*]

Ambassador	There is, of late, news come unto the court
	That old lord Leir remains in Cambria.
	I'll hie me thither presently to impart
	My letters and my message unto him.
	I never was less welcome to a place
	In all my lifetime than I have been hither,
	Especially unto the stately queen
	Who would not cast one gracious look on me,
	But still with louring and suspicious eyes
	Would take exceptions at each word I spake, 10

And fain she would have undermined me
To know what my ambassage did import.
But she is like to hop without her hope
And in this matter for to want her will,
Though, by report, she'll have't in all things else.
Well, I will post away for Cambria;
Within these few days I hope to be there. *Exit*

[5.1]

Enter the King of GALLIA, [CORDELLA] *and* MUMFORD

Gallia   By this, our father understands our mind
And our kind greetings sent to him of late;
Therefore, my mind presageth, ere't be long
We shall receive from Britain happy news.

Cordella   I fear my sister will dissuade his mind,
For she to me hath always been unkind.

Gallia   Fear not, my love, since that we know the worst,
The last means helps if that we miss the first:
If he'll not come to Gallia unto us,
Then we will sail to Britain unto him   10

Mumford   Well, if I once see Britain again, I have sworn I'll
ne'er come home without my wench, and I'll not be
forsworn. I'll rather never come home while I live.

Cordella   Are you sure, Mumford, she is a maid still?

Mumford   Nay, I'll not swear she is a maid, but she goes for one.
I'll take her at all adventures if I can get her.

Cordella   Ay, that's well put in.

Mumford   Well put in? Nay, it was ill put in, for had it been as
well put in as e'er I put in in my days, I would have
made her follow me to France.   20

Cordella	Nay, you'd have been so kind as take her with you, or else, were I as she, I would have been so loving as I'd stay behind you. Yet I must confess, you are a very proper man and able to make a wench do more than she would do.
Mumford	Well, I have a pair of slops for the nonce will hold all your mocks.
Gallia	Nay, we see you have a handsome hose.
Cordella	Ay, and of the newest fashion.
Mumford	More bobs, more. Put them in still; they'll serve 30 instead of bombast! Yet put not in too many, lest the seams crack and they fly out amongst you again. You must not think to outface me so easily in my mistress' quarrel, who, if I see once again, ten team of horses shall not draw me away till I have full and whole possession.
Gallia	Ay, but one team and a cart will serve the turn.
Cordella	Not only for him, but also for his wench.
Mumford	Well, you are two to one; I'll give you over. And since I see you so pleasantly disposed, which 40 indeed is but seldom seen, I'll claim a promise of you which you shall not deny me: for promise is debt, and by this hand you promised it me, therefore you owe it me, and you shall pay it me, or I'll sue you upon an action of unkindness.
Gallia	Prithee, proud Mumford, what promise did I make thee?
Mumford	Faith, nothing but this: that the next fair weather, which is very now, you would go in progress down to the seaside, which is very near.

Gallia	Faith, in this motion I will join with thee,	50

Gallia   Faith, in this motion I will join with thee,   50
                And be a mediator to my queen.
                Prithee, my love, let this match go forward;
                My mind foretells 'twill be a lucky voyage

Cordella   Entreaty needs not where you may command.
                So you be pleas'd, I am right well content.
                Yet, as the sea I much desire to see,
                So am I most unwilling to be seen.

Gallia   We'll go disguised, all unknown to any.

Cordella   Howsoever you make one, I'll make another.

Mumford   And I the third. Oh, I am overjoyed!   60
                See what love is, which getteth with a word
                What all the world besides could ne'er obtain!
                But what disguises shall we have, my lord?

Gallia   Faith thus: my queen and I will be disguis'd
                Like a plain country couple, and you shall be Roger,
                Our man, and wait upon us – or, if you will,
                You shall go first, and we will wait on you.

Mumford   'Twere more than time. This device is excellent!
                Come let us about it.   *Exeunt*

[5.2]
                Enter [the King of] CAMBRIA *and* RAGAN, *with Nobles*

Cambria   What strange mischance or unexpected hap
                Hath thus depriv'd us of our father's presence?
                Can no man tell us what's become of him,
                With whom we did converse not two days since?
                My lords, let everywhere light horse be sent
                To scour about through all our regiment;
                Dispatch a post immediately to Cornwall

	To see if any news be of him there;	
	Myself will make a strict inquiry here,	
	And all about our cities near at hand,	10
	Till certain news of his abode be brought.	

Ragan   All sorrow is but counterfeit to mine,
Whose lips are almost sealed up with grief.
Mine is the substance, whilst they do but seem
To weep the loss, which tears cannot redeem.
Oh, ne'er was heard so strange a misadventure,
A thing so far beyond the reach of sense,
Since no man's reason in the cause can enter.
What hath remov'd my father thus from hence?
Oh, I do fear some charm or invocation   20
Of wicked spirits or infernal fiends
Stirr'd by Cordella moves this innovation,
And brings my father timeless to his end.
But, might I know that the detested witch
Were certain cause of this uncertain ill,
Myself to France would go in some disguise
And with these nails scratch out her hateful eyes.
For since I am deprived of my father,
I loathe my life and wish my death the rather.

Cambria   The heav'ns are just and hate impiety,   30
And will, no doubt, reveal such heinous crimes.
Censure not any till you know the right;
Let him be judge that bringeth truth to light.

Ragan   Oh, but my grief, like to a swelling tide,
Exceeds the bounds of common patience,
Nor can I moderate my tongue so much
To conceal them whom I hold in suspect.

Cambria   This matter shall be sifted: if't be she,

A thousand Frances shall not harbour her.

Enter the Gallian AMBASSADOR

Ambassador	All happiness unto the Cambrian king.	40
Cambria	Welcome, my friend. From whence is thy ambassage?	
Ambassador	I came from Gallia, unto Cornwall sent With letters to your honourable father, Whom there not finding, as I did expect, I was directed hither to repair.	
Ragan	Frenchman, what is thy message to my father?	
Ambassador	My letters, madam, will import the same, Which my commission is for to deliver.	
Ragan	In's absence you may trust us with your letters.	
Ambassador	I must perform my charge in such a manner As I have strict commandment from the king.	50
Ragan	There is good packing 'twixt your king and you. You need not hither come to ask for him; You know where he is better than ourselves.	
Ambassador	Madam, I hope, not far off.	
Ragan	Hath the young murd'ress, your outrageous queen, No means to colour her detested deeds In finishing my guiltless father's days – Because he gave her nothing to her dower – But, by the colour of a fain'd ambassage, To send him letters hither to our court? Go carry them to them that sent them hither And bid them keep their scrolls unto themselves. They cannot blind us with such slight excuse, To smother up so monstrous vile abuse.	60

	And, were it not it is 'gainst law of arms	
	To offer violence to a messenger,	
	We would inflict such torments on thyself	
	As should enforce thee to reveal the truth.	
Ambassador	Madam, your threats no whit appal my mind.	70
	I know my conscience guiltless of this act.	
	My king and queen, I dare be sworn, are free	
	From any thought of such impiety;	
	And therefore, madam, you have done them wrong,	
	And ill-beseeming with a sister's love,	
	Who in mere duty tender him as much	
	As ever you respected him for dower.	
	The king your husband will not say as much.	
Cambria	I will suspend my judgement for a time	
	Till more appearance give us further light,	80
	Yet, to be plain, your coming doth enforce	
	A great suspicion to our doubtful mind,	
	And that you do resemble, to be brief,	
	Him that first robs and then cries 'stop the thief!'	
Ambassador	Pray God some near you have not done the like.	
Ragan	Hence, saucy mate: reply no more to us,	(*strikes him*)
	For law of arms shall not protect thy tongue.	
Ambassador	Ne'er was I offer'd such discourtesy.	
	God and my king, I trust, ere it be long,	90
	Will find a mean to remedy this wrong.	*Exit*
Ragan	How shall I live to suffer this disgrace	
	At every base and vulgar peasant's hands?	
	It ill-befitteth my imperial state	
	To be thus used, and no man take my part.	(*Weeps*)
Cambria	What should I do? Infringe the law of arms	

Were to my everlasting obloquy,
But I will take revenge upon his master
Which sent him hither to delude us thus.

Ragan   Nay, if you put up this, be sure, ere long,
          Now that my father thus is made away,   100
          She'll come and claim a third part of your crown
          As due unto her by inheritance.

Cambria   But I will prove her title to be nought
          But shame and the reward of parricide,
          And make her an example to the world
          For after-ages to admire her penance.
          This will I do, as I am Cambria's king,
          Or lose my life to prosecute revenge.
          Come, first let's learn what news is of our father   109
          And then proceed as best occasion fits.   *Exeunt*

[5.3]
              Enter LEIR, PERILLUS, and two MARINERS, in sea-gowns
                              and sea-caps

Perillus My honest friends, we are asham'd to show
          The great extremity of our present state,
          In that, at this time, we are brought so low
          That we want money for to pay our passage.
          The truth is so: we met with some 'good fellows'
          A little before we came aboard your ship,
          Which strip'd us quite of all the coin we had
          And left us not a penny in our purses.
          Yet, wanting money, we will use the mean
          To see you satisfied to the uttermost.   10

1 Mariner (*look[s] on LEIR*) Here's a good gown; 'twould

become me passing well! I should be fine in it.

2 Mariner (*look*[*s*] *on* PERILLUS) Here's a good cloak. I marvel how I should look in it.

Leir Faith, had we others to supply their room,
Though ne'er so mean, you willingly should have them.

1 Mariner Do you hear, sir? You look like an honest man; I'll not stand to do you a pleasure. Here's a good strong motley gaberdine, cost me fourteen good shillings at Billingsgate. Give me your gown for it, and your cap for mine, and I'll forgive your passage.

Leir With all my heart, and twenty thanks.

LEIR *and* [1 MARINER *ex*]*change* [*clothes*]

2 Mariner Do you hear, sir? You shall have a better match than he, because you are my friend. Here is a good sheep's russet sea-gown will bide more stress, I warrant you, than two of his; yet, for you seem to be an honest gentleman, I am content to change it for your cloak, and ask you nothing for your passage more. (*Pull*[*s*] *off* PERILLUS's *cloak*)

Perillus My own I willingly would change with thee
And think myself indebted to thy kindness –
But would my friend might keep his garment still!
My friend, I'll give thee this new doublet, if thou'lt
Restore his gown unto him back again.

1 Mariner Nay, if I do, would I might ne'er eat powder'd beef and mustard more, nor drink can of good liquor whilst I live. My friend, you have small reason to seek to hinder me of my bargain, but the best is: a bargain's a bargain.

Leir	([*aside*] *to* PERILLUS) Kind friend, it is much better as it is,
	For by this means we may escape unknown 40
	Till time and opportunity do fit.
2 Mariner	Hark, hark, they are laying their heads together;
	they'll repent them of their bargain anon; 'twere
	best for us to go while we are well.
1 Mariner	God be with you, sir; for your passage back again,
	I'll use you as unreasonable as another.
Leir	I know thou wilt, but we hope to bring ready
	money with us when we come back again.

Exeunt Mariners

	Were ever men in this extremity:
	In a strange country, and devoid of friends, 50
	And not a penny for to help ourselves?
	Kind friend, what think'st thou will become of us?
Perillus	Be of good cheer, my lord! I have a doublet
	Will yield us money enough to serve our turns
	Until we come unto your daughter's court,
	And then, I hope, we shall find friends enough.
Leir	Ah, kind Perillus, that is it I fear,
	And makes me faint or ever I come there.
	Can kindness spring out of ingratitude?
	Or love be reap'd where hatred hath been sown? 60
	Can henbane join in league with mithridate?
	Or sugar grow in wormwood's bitter stalk?
	It cannot be; they are too opposite –
	And so am I to any kindness here.
	I have thrown wormwood on the sugar'd youth,
	And like to henbane poisoned the fount
	Whence flow'd the mithridate of a child's good will.

I, like an envious thorn, have prick'd the heart
And turn'd sweet grapes to sour unrelish'd sloes.
The causeless ire of my respectless breast   70
Hath sour'd the sweet milk of dame Nature's paps.
My bitter words have gall'd her honey thoughts,
And weeds of rancour chok'd the flower of grace.
Then what remainder is of any hope,
But all our fortunes will go quite aslope?

Perillus   Fear not, my lord, the perfect good indeed
             Can never be corrupted by the bad.
             A new fresh vessel still retains the taste
             Of that which first is pour'd into the same,
             And therefore, though you name yourself the thorn,   80
             The weed, the gall, the henbane and the wormwood,
             Yet she'll continue in her former state,
             The honey, milk, grape, sugar, mithridate.

Leir   Thou pleasing orator unto me in woe,
             Cease to beguile me with thy hopeful speeches.
             Oh, join with me and think of nought but crosses,
             And then we'll one lament another's losses.

Perillus   Why, say the worst: the worst can be but death,
             And death is better than for to despair.
             Then hazard death, which may convert to life;   90
             Banish despair, which brings a thousand deaths.

Leir   O'ercome with thy strong arguments, I yield
             To be directed by thee as thou wilt.
             As thou yield'st comfort to my crazed thoughts,
             Would I could yield the like unto thy body,
             Which is full weak, I know, and ill apaid,
             For want of fresh meat and due sustenance.

Perillus   Alack, my lord, my heart doth bleed to think

That you should be in such extremity.

Leir   Come, let us go and see what God will send;   100
                When all means fail, He is the surest friend.   *Exeunt*

[5.4]
                Enter the King of GALLIA[, CORDELLA], *and* MUMFORD, *with a*
                basket, disguised like country folk

Gallia   This tedious journey all on foot, sweet love,
                Cannot be pleasing to your tender joints,
                Which ne'er were used to these toilsome walks.

Cordella   I never in my life took more delight
                In any journey than I do in this.
                It did me good, whenas we happ'd to light
                Amongst the merry crew of country folk,
                To see what industry and pains they took
                To win them commendations 'mongst their friends.
                Lord, how they labour to bestir themselves   10
                And, in their quirks, to go beyond the moon,
                And so take on them with such antic fits
                That one would think they were beside their wits!
                Come away, Roger, with your basket.

Mumford   Soft, dame, here comes a couple of old youths.
                I must needs make myself fat with jesting at them.

                Enter LEIR *and* PERILLUS *very faintly*

Cordella   Nay, prithee do not! They do seem to be
                Men much o'ergone with grief and misery.
                Let's stand aside and hearken what they say.

Leir   Ah, my Perillus, now I see we both   20
                Shall end our days in this unfruitful soil.
                Oh, I do faint for want of sustenance,

And thou, I know, in little better case.
No gentle tree affords one taste of fruit
To comfort us until we meet with men;
No lucky path conducts our luckless steps
Unto a place where any comfort dwells.
Sweet rest betide unto our happy souls,
For here I see our bodies must have end!

Perillus   Ah, my dear lord, how doth my heart lament   30
To see you brought to this extremity!
Oh, if you love me as you do profess,
Or ever thought well of me in my life,   (*strips up his arm*)
Feed on this flesh, whose veins are not so dry
But there is virtue left to comfort you!
Oh, feed on this; if this will do you good,
I'll smile for joy to see you suck my blood.

Leir   I am no cannibal, that I should delight
To slake my hungry jaws with human flesh;
I am no devil, or ten times worse than so,   40
To suck the blood of such a peerless friend.
Oh, do not think that I respect my life
So dearly as I do thy loyal love.
Ah, Britain, I shall never see thee more,
That hast unkindly banished thy king –
And yet not thou dost make me to complain,
But they which were more near to me than thou.

Cordella   [*aside*] What do I hear? This lamentable voice
Methinks, ere now, I oftentimes have heard.

Leir   Ah, Gonoril, was half my kingdom's gift   50
The cause that thou didst seek to have my life?
Ah, cruel Ragan, did I give thee all,
And all could not suffice without my blood?

Ah, poor Cordella, did I give thee nought,
Nor never shall be able for to give?
Oh, let me warn all ages that ensu'th,
How they trust flatt'ry and reject the truth.
Well, unkind girls, I here forgive you both,
Yet the just heav'ns will hardly do the like,
And only crave forgiveness at the end   60
Of good Cordella, and of thee, my friend –
Of God, whose majesty I have offended
By my transgression many thousand ways;
Of her, dear heart, whom I for no occasion
Turn'd out of all, through flatterers' persuasion;
Of thee, kind friend who, but for me, I know,
Had'st never come unto this place of woe.

Cordella   Alack, that ever I should live to see
My noble father in this misery.

Gallia   Sweet love, reveal not what thou art as yet,   70
Until we know the ground of all this ill.

Cordella   Oh, but some meat, some meat! Do you not see
How near they are to death for want of food?
             [*Takes* MUMFORD'S *basket and empties out the food*]

Perillus   Lord, which didst help thy servants at their need,
Or now or never send us help with speed!
[*Sees the food*] Oh, comfort, comfort! Yonder is a banquet,
And men and women! My lord, be of good cheer,
For I see comfort coming very near!
Oh, my lord, a banquet, and men and women!

Leir   Oh, let kind pity mollify their hearts   80
That they may help us in our great extremes.

Perillus   God save you, friends! And if this blessed banquet

Affordeth any food or sustenance,
E'en for His sake that saved us all from death,
Vouchsafe to save us from the grip of famine.

Cordella   (*bring[s] him to the table*)
Here father, sit and eat! Here, sit and drink!
And would it were far better for your sakes.

Perillus   (*takes* LEIR *by the hand to the table*)
I'll give you thanks anon; my friend doth faint
And needeth present comfort.

                                                           LEIR *drinks*

Mumford   I warrant he ne'er stays to say grace. Oh, there's no   90
               sauce to a good stomach.

Perillus   The blessed God of heaven hath thought upon us.

Leir   The thanks be His, and these kind courteous folk,
               By whose humanity we are preserved.

                   [LEIR *and* PERILLUS] *eat hungrily*, [*then*] LEIR *drinks*

Cordella   And may that draught be unto him, as was
               That which old Aeson drank, which did renew
               His withered age and made him young again.
               And may that meat be unto him as was
               That which Elias ate, in strength whereof
               He walked forty days and never fainted.   100
               Shall I conceal me longer from my father
               Or shall I manifest myself to him?

Gallia   Forbear awhile until his strength return
               Lest, being overjoyed with seeing thee,
               His poor weak senses should forsake their office,
               And so our cause of joy be turn'd to sorrow.

Perillus	What cheer, my lord? How do you feel yourself?
Leir	Methinks I never ate such savoury meat:
	It is as pleasant as the blessed manna
	That rain'd from heaven amongst the Israelites. 110
	It hath recall'd my spirits home again
	And made me fresh as erst I was before.
	But how shall we congratulate their kindness?
Perillus	In faith, I know not how sufficiently,
	But the best mean that I can think on is this:
	I'll offer them my doublet in requital,
	For we have nothing else to spare.
Leir	Nay, stay, Perillus, for they shall have mine!
Perillus	Pardon, my lord, I swear they shall have mine!
	(Proffers his doublet[;] they will not take it)
Leir	Ah, who would think such kindness should remain 120
	Among such strange and unacquainted men,
	And that such hate should harbour in the breast
	Of those which have occasion to be best?
Cordella	Ah, good old father, tell to me thy grief;
	I'll sorrow with thee if not add relief.
Leir	Ah, good young daughter – I may call thee so,
	For thou art like a daughter I did owe.
Cordella	Do you not owe her still? What, is she dead?
Leir	No, God forbid. But all my interest's gone,
	By showing myself too much unnatural. 130
	So have I lost the title of a father,
	And may be call'd a stranger to her rather.
Cordella	Your title's good still; for 'tis always known
	A man may do as him list with his own.

	But have you but one daughter then in all?
Leir	Yes, I have more by two than would I had.
Cordella	Oh, say not so, but rather see the end:
	They that are bad may have the grace to mend.
	But how have they offended you so much?
Leir	If from the first I should relate the cause, 140
	'Twould make a heart of adamant to weep;
	And thou, poor soul, kind-hearted as thou art,
	Dost weep already ere I do begin.
Cordella	For God's love, tell it! And, when you have done,
	I'll tell the reason why I weep so soon.
Leir	Then know this first. I am a Briton born,
	And had three daughters by one loving wife;
	And, though I say it, of beauty they were sped,
	Especially the youngest of the three,
	For her perfections hardly match'd could be. 150
	On these I doted with a jealous love,
	And thought to try which of them lov'd me best
	By asking them which would do most for me.
	The first and second flatter'd me with words,
	And vow'd they lov'd me better than their lives;
	The youngest said she loved me as a child
	Might do: her answer I esteem'd most vild,
	And presently in an outrageous mood
	I turn'd her from me to go sink or swim;
	And all I had, e'en to the very clothes, 160
	I gave in dowry with the other two –
	And she, that best deserv'd the greatest share,
	I gave her nothing but disgrace and care.
	Now mark the sequel. When I had done thus,
	I sojourn'd in my eldest daughter's house

Where, for a time, I was entreated well
And liv'd in state sufficing my content.
But every day her kindness did grow cold,
Which I, with patience, put up well enough,
And seemed not to see the things I saw;   170
But, at the last, she grew so far incens'd
With moody fury and with causeless hate
That in most vile and contumelious terms,
She bade me pack and harbour somewhere else.
Then was I fain for refuge to repair
Unto my other daughter for relief,
Who gave me pleasing and most courteous words,
But in her actions showed herself so sore
As never any daughter did before.
She pray'd me in a morning out betime   180
To go to a thicket two miles from the court,
Pointing that there she would come talk with me.
There she had set a shag-hair'd, murd'ring wretch
To massacre my honest friend and me!
Then judge yourself, although my tale be brief,
If ever man had greater cause of grief.

Gallia   Nor never like impiety was done
Since the creation of the world begun.

Leir   And now I am constrain'd to seek relief
Of her, to whom I have been so unkind,   190
Whose censure, if it do award me death,
I must confess she pays me but my due.
But if she show a loving daughter's part,
It comes of God and her, not my desert.

Cordella   No doubt she will. I dare be sworn she will!

Leir   How know you that, not knowing what she is?

Cordella	Myself a father have a great way hence,
	Us'd me as ill as ever you did her;
	Yet, that his reverend age I once might see,
	I'd creep along to meet him on my knee. 200
Leir	Oh, no men's children are unkind but mine!
Cordella	Condemn not all because of others' crime
	But, look, dear father! Look, behold, and see:
	Thy loving daughter speaketh unto thee! (*Kneels*)
Leir	Oh, stand thou up; ([CORDELLA *rises as*] *he kneels*)
	it is my part to kneel
	And ask forgiveness for my former faults.
Cordella	Oh, if you wish I should enjoy my breath,
	Dear father rise, or I receive my death.
Leir	Then I will rise to satisfy your mind,
	(*rise*[*s and then immediately*] *kneel*[*s again*])
	But kneel again till pardon be resign'd. 210
Cordella	I pardon you? The word beseems not me,
	But I do say so for to ease your knee.
	You gave me life; you were the cause that I
	Am what I am, who else had never been.
Leir	But you gave life to me and to my friend,
	Whose days had else had an untimely end.
Cordella	You brought me up whenas I was but young
	And far unable for to help myself.
Leir	I cast thee forth, whenas thou wast but young
	And far unable for to help thyself. 220
Cordella	God, world, and nature say I do you wrong
	That can endure to see you kneel so long.

Gallia	Let me break off this loving controversy, Which doth rejoice my very soul to see. Good father, rise. She is your loving daughter ([LEIR] *rises*) And honours you with as respective duty As if you were the monarch of the world.

Cordella   (*kneels*) But I will never rise from off my knee
Until I have your blessing and your pardon
Of all my faults committed any way   230
From my first birth unto this present day.

Leir   The blessing which the God of Abraham gave
Unto the tribe of Judah light on thee
And multiply thy days, that thou mayst see
Thy children's children prosper after thee.
Thy faults which are just – none that I do know –
God pardon on high and I forgive below.

Cordella   (*rises*) Now is my heart at quiet, and doth leap
Within my breast for joy of this good hap.
And now, dear father, welcome to our court,   240
And welcome, kind Perillus, unto me,
Mirror of virtue and true honesty.

Leir   Oh, he hath been the kindest friend to me
That ever man had in adversity.

Perillus   My tongue doth fail to say what heart doth think,
I am so ravish'd with exceeding joy.

Gallia   All you have spoke. Now let me speak my mind,
And in few words much matter here conclude:
(*kneels*) If e'er my heart do harbour any joy,
Or true content repose within my breast,   .   250
Till I have rooted out this viperous sect

	And repossess'd my father of his crown,	
	Let me be counted for the perjur'dst man	
	That ever spake word since the world began.	(*Rises*)
Mumford	Let me pray, too, that never pray'd before:	
	(*kneels*) If e'er I resalute the British earth –	
	As, ere't be long, I do presume I shall –	
	And do return from thence without my wench,	
	Let me be gelded for my recompense.	(*Rises*)
Gallia	Come, let's to arms for to redress this wrong;	260
	Till I am there, methinks the time seems long.	*Exeunt*

[5.5]

Enter RAGAN

Ragan	I feel a hell of conscience in my breast	
	Tormenting me with horror for my fact,	
	And makes me in an agony of doubt,	
	For fear the world should find my dealing out.	
	The slave, whom I appointed for the act,	
	I ne'er set eye upon the peasant since.	
	Oh, could I get him for to make him sure,	
	My doubts would cease and I should rest secure.	
	But if the old men, with persuasive words,	
	Have sav'd their lives and made him to relent,	10
	Then are they fled unto the court of France	
	And like a trumpet manifest my shame.	
	A shame on these white-liver'd slaves, say I,	
	That with fair words so soon are overcome.	
	O God, that I had been but made a man,	
	Or that my strength were equal with my will!	
	These foolish men are nothing but mere pity,	
	And melt as butter doth against the sun.	

Why should they have pre-eminence over us,
Since we are creatures of more brave resolve?   20
I swear, I am quite out of charity
With all the heartless men in Christendom!
A pox upon them when they are afraid
To give a stab or slit a paltry wind-pipe,
Which are so easy matters to be done.
Well, had I thought the slave would serve me so,
Myself would have been executioner.
'Tis now undone, and if that it be known,
I'll make as good shift as I can for one.
He that repines at me, howe'er it stands,   30
'Twere best for him to keep him from my hands.   *Exit*

[5.6]

Sound drums and trumpets; enter the King of GALLIA, LEIR,
MUMFORD *and the army*

Gallia   Thus have we brought our army to the sea,
                Whereas our ships are ready to receive us.
                The wind stands fair, and we in four hours' sail
                May easily arrive on British shore
                Where, unexpected, we may them surprise
                And gain a glorious victory with ease.
                Wherefore, my loving countrymen, resolve,
                Since truth and justice fighteth on our sides,
                That we shall march with conquest where we go.
                Myself will be as forward as the first,   10
                And step-by-step march with the hardiest wight,
                And not the meanest soldier in our camp
                Shall be in danger but I'll second him.
                To you, my lord, we give the whole command
                Of all the army, next unto ourself,

Not doubting of you, but you will extend
Your wonted valour in this needful case,
Encouraging the rest to do the like
By your approved magnanimity.

Mumford   My liege, 'tis needless to spur a willing horse   20
That's apt enough to run himself to death:
For here I swear by that sweet saint's bright eyes,
Which are the stars which guide me to good hap,
Either to see my old lord crown'd anew,
Or in his cause to bid the world adieu.

Leir   Thanks, good lord Mumford, 'tis more of your good will
Than any merit or desert in me.

Mumford   And now to you, my worthy countrymen,
Ye valiant race of Cenovestan Gauls
Surnamed Redshanks for your chivalry,   30
Because you fight up to the shanks in blood –
Show yourselves now to be right Gauls indeed
And be so bitter on your enemies
That they may say you are as bitter as gall.
Gall them, brave shot, with your artillery!
Gall them, brave halberds, with your sharp-point bills
Each in their 'pointed place; not one but all
Fight for the credit of yourselves and Gaul!

Gallia   Then what should more persuasion need to those
That rather wish to deal than hear of blows?   40
Let's to our ships, and if that God permit,
In four hours' sail I hope we shall be there.

Mumford   And in five hours more, I make no doubt,
But we shall bring our wish'd desires about.   *Exeunt*

[5.7]

    Enter [1 CAPTAIN,] *a captain of the watch, and two* WATCHMEN

1 Captain	My honest friends, it is your turn tonight
	To watch in this place near about the beacon
	And vigilantly have regard
	If any fleet of ships pass hitherward,
	Which, if you do, your office is to fire
	The beacon presently and raise the town. *Exit*
1 Watchman	Ay, ay, ay, fear nothing. We know our charge, I
	warrant. I have been a watchman about this beacon
	this thirty year, and yet I ne'er see it stir but stood
	as quietly as might be. 10
2 Watchman	Faith, neighbour, an you'll follow my 'vice,
	instead of watching the beacon, we'll go to
	goodman Jennings and watch a pot of ale and a
	rasher of bacon. An if we do not drink ourselves
	drunk, then, so I warrant, the beacon will see us
	when we come out again.
1 Watchman	Ay, but how if somebody excuse us to the captain?
2 Watchman	'Tis no matter: I'll prove by good reason that we
	watch the beacon, as, for example –
1 Watchman	I hope you do not call me 'ass' by craft, neighbour. 20
2 Watchman	No, no, but for example. Say here stands the pot of
	ale: that's the beacon.
1 Watchman	Ay, ay, 'tis a very good beacon.
2 Watchman	Well, say here stands your nose: that's the fire.
1 Watchman	Indeed, I must confess 'tis somewhat red.
2 Watchman	I see come marching in a dish half-a-score pieces of

salt bacon.

1 Watchman	I understand your meaning; that's as much as to say, half a score ships.
2 Watchman	True, you conster right. Presently, like a faithful 30 watchman, I fire the beacon and call up the town.
1 Watchman	Ay, that's as much as to say: you set your nose to the pot and drink up the drink.
2 Watchman	You are in the right; come, let's go fire the beacon. *Exeunt*

[5.8]

    Enter the King of GALLIA *with a still march,* MUMFORD *and soldiers*

Gallia	Now march our ensigns on the British earth,
	And we are near-approaching to the town.
	Then look about you, valiant countrymen,
	And we shall finish this exploit with ease.
	Th'inhabitants of this mistrustful place
	Are dead asleep, as men that are secure.
	Here shall we skirmish but with naked men,
	Devoid of sense, new-waked from a dream,
	That know not what our coming doth portend
	Till they do feel our meaning on their skins. 10
	Therefore, assail! God and our right for us! *Exeunt*

[5.9]

    Alarum, with men and women half naked[.] Enter two CAPTAINS
                  without doublets, with swords

1 Captain	Where are these villains, that were set to watch
	And fire the beacon if occasion serv'd,
	That thus have suffer'd us to be surpris'd
	And never given notice to the town?

We are betray'd and quite devoid of hope
By any means to fortify ourselves.

2 Captain 'Tis ten to one the peasants are o'ercome
With drink and sleep, and so neglect their charge.

1 Captain A whirlwind carry them quick to a whirlpool,
That there the slaves may drink their bellies full. 10

2 Captain This 'tis, to have the beacon so near the ale-house.

Enter the WATCHMEN *drunk, with each a pot*

1 Captain Out on ye, villains! Whither run you now?

1 Watchman To fire the town and call up the beacon!

2 Watchman No, no, sir, to fire the beacon. (*Drinks*)

2 Captain What, with a pot of ale? You drunken rogues!

1 Captain You'll 'fire the beacon' when the town is lost!
I'll teach you how to tend your office better!

(*Draws to stab them*)

Enter MUMFORD[.] CAPTAINS *run away*

Mumford Yield, yield, yield! (*Kicks down their pots*)

1 Watchman Reel? No, we do not reel! You may lack a pot of
ale ere you die! 20

Mumford But in mean space I answer: you want none. Well,
there's no dealing with you. Y'are tall men and
well-weapon'd; I would there were no worse than
you in the town. *Exit*

2 Watchman 'A speaks like an honest man; my choler's past
already. Come, neighbour, let's go.

1 Watchman	Nay, first let's see an we can stand. *Exeunt*

Alarum, excursions, MUMFORD *after them, and some half naked.*

[5.10]
Enter the King of GALLIA, LEIR, MUMFORD, CORDELLA,
PERILLUS, [*British* NOBLEMAN] *and soldiers, with the chief of the
town bound*

Gallia Fear not, my friends, you shall receive no hurt
If you'll subscribe unto your lawful king
And quite revoke your fealty from Cambria
And from aspiring Cornwall too, whose wives
Have practis'd treason 'gainst their father's life.
We come in justice of your wronged king,
And do intend no harm at all to you,
So you submit unto your lawful king.

Leir Kind countrymen, it grieves me that, perforce,
I am constrain'd to use extremities.   10

Nobleman Long have you here been look'd for, good my lord,
And wish'd for by a general consent;
And had we known your highness had arriv'd,
We had not made resistance to your grace.
And now, my gracious lord, you need not doubt
But all the country will yield presently,
Which, since your absence, have been greatly tax'd
For to maintain their overswelling pride.
We'll presently send word to all our friends;
When they have notice, they will come apace.   20

Leir Thanks, loving subjects; and thanks, worthy son;

Thanks, my kind daughter; thanks to you, my lord,
Who willingly adventur'd have your blood,
Without desert, to do me so much good.

Mumford   Oh, say not so: I have been much beholding to your
grace! I must confess, I have been in some
skirmishes, but I was never in the like to this – for
where I was wont to meet with armed men, I was
now encounter'd with naked women.

Cordella   We that are feeble and want use of arms   30
Will pray to God to shield you from all harms.

Leir   The while your hands do manage ceaseless toil,
Our hearts shall pray the foes may have the foil.

Perillus   We'll fast and pray, whilst you for us do fight,
That victory may prosecute the right.

Gallia   Methinks your words do amplify, my friends,
And add fresh vigour to my willing limbs.

                                [*Sound a*] *drum*

But hark, I hear the adverse drum approach.
God and our right, Saint Denis, and Saint George!

Enter CORNWALL, CAMBRIA, GONORIL, RAGAN, *and the army*

Cornwall   Presumptuous king of Gauls, how darest thou   40
Presume to enter on our British shore?
And more than that, to take our towns perforce
And draw our subjects' hearts from their true king?
Be sure to buy it at as dear a price
As e'er you bought presumption in your lives.

Gallia   O'er-daring Cornwall, know we come in right
And just revengement of the wronged king,
Whose daughters there, fell vipers as they are,

	Have sought to murder and deprive of life;	
	But God protected him from all their spite,	50
	And we are come in justice of his right.	
Cambria	Nor he nor thou have any interest here	
	But what you win and purchase with the sword.	
	Thy slanders to our noble, virtuous queens	
	We'll in the battle thrust them down thy throat,	
	Except, for fear of our revenging hands,	
	Thou fly to sea as not secure on lands.	
Mumford	Welshman, I'll so ferret you ere night for that word,	
	that you shall have no mind to crake so well this	
	twelvemonth.	60
Gonoril	They lie that say we sought our father's death.	
Ragan	'Tis merely forged for a colour's sake	
	To set a gloss on your invasion.	
	Methinks an old man ready for to die	
	Should be asham'd to broach so foul a lie.	
Cordella	Fie, shameless sister, so devoid of grace	
	To call our father liar to his face.	
Gonoril	Peace, puritan! Dissembling hypocrite,	
	Which art so good that thou wilt prove stark naught.	
	Anon, whenas I have you in my fingers,	70
	I'll make you wish yourself in purgatory.	
Perillus	Nay, peace, thou monster! Shame unto thy sex!	
	Thou fiend in likeness of a humane creature!	
Ragan	I never heard a fouler-spoken man!	
Leir	Out on thee, viper! Scum! Filthy parricide!	
	More odious to my sight than is a toad!	
	Knowest thou these letters?	

Ragan	*(snatches them and tears them)*
	Think you to outface me with your paltry scrolls?
	You come to drive my husband from his right
	Under the colour of a forged letter. 80
Leir	Who ever heard the like impiety?
Perillus	You are our debtor of more patience;
	We were more patient when we stay'd for you
	Within the thicket two long hours and more.
Ragan	What hours? What thicket?
Perillus	There, where you sent your servant with your letters,
	Seal'd with your hand, to send us both to heaven
	Where, as I think, you never mean to come.
Ragan	Alas, you are grown a child again with age,
	Or else your senses dote for want of sleep. 90
Perillus	Indeed you made us rise betimes, you know;
	Yet had a care we should sleep where you bade us stay,
	But never wake more till the latter day.
Gonoril	Peace, peace, old fellow; thou art sleepy still!
Mumford	Faith, an if you reason till tomorrow, you get no other
	answer at their hands. 'Tis pity two such good faces
	should have so little grace between them. Well –
	Let us see if their husbands with their hands,
	Can do as much as they do with their tongues. 99
Cambria	Ay, with their swords they'll make your tongues unsay
	What they have said, or else they'll cut them out.
Gallia	To't, gallants, to't, let's not stand brawling thus.

Exeunt both armies

[5.11]

Sound alarum; excursions. MUMFORD [*chases*] CAMBRIA *away;*
then [*alarums*] *cease.*

Enter CORNWALL

Cornwall   The day is lost; our friends do all revolt
            And join against us with the adverse part.
            There is no means of safety but by flight,
            And therefore I'll to Cornwall with my queen.   *Exit*

Enter CAMBRIA

Cambria   I think there is a devil in the camp hath haunted me
            today; he hath so tired me that in a manner I can
            fight no more.

Enter MUMFORD

            Zounds, here he comes! I'll take me to my horse!   *Exit*

            MUMFORD *follows him to the door, and returns*

Mumford   Farewell, Welshman! Give thee but thy due:
            Thou hast a light and nimble pair of legs –
            Thou are more in debt to them than to thy hands –   10
            But if I meet thee once again today,
            I'll cut them off and set them to a better heart.   *Exit*

            Alarums and excursions, then [*musicians*] *sound victory.*

Enter LEIR, PERILLUS, GALLIA, CORDELLA, *and* MUMFORD

Gallia   Thanks be to God, your foes are overcome
            And you again possessed of your right.

Leir   First to the heav'ns, next thanks to you, my son,
            By whose good means I repossess the same,
            Which, if it please you to accept yourself,
            With all my heart I will resign to you –

For it is yours by right, and none of mine.
First have you rais'd, at your own charge, a power   20
Of valiant soldiers – this comes all from you –
Next have you ventur'd your own person's scathe,
And, lastly, worthy Gallia never stain'd
My kingly title I by thee have gain'd.

Gallia   Thank heav'ns, not me: my zeal to you is such,
Command my utmost, I will never grutch.

Cordella   He that with all kind love entreats his queen
Will not be to her father unkind seen.

Leir   Ah, my Cordella, now I call to mind
The modest answer which I took unkind.   30
But now I see I am no whit beguil'd:
Thou lov'dst me dearly, and as ought a child.
And thou, Perillus, partner once in woe,
Thee to requite the best I can I'll do.
Yet all I can, ay, were it ne'er so much,
Were not sufficient, thy true love is such.
Thanks, worthy Mumford, to thee last of all,
Not greeted last 'cause thy desert was small:
No! Thou hast lion-like laid on today,
Chasing the Cornwall king and Cambria   40
Who, with my daughters – daughters did I say? –
To save their lives, the fugitives did play.
Come, son and daughter, who did me advance,
Repose with me awhile and then for France.

Sound drums and trumpets

Exeunt

FINIS

GLOSSARIAL NOTES

1.1

1	*our* my – Leir uses the 'royal we' throughout this and many of his following speeches.
	Obsequies funeral rites
4	*cherubims* an order or company of angels; the Hebrew plural is 'cherubim'.
8-9	*For whom ... their states* nature makes me especially concerned to advance them
10	*wanting* a) lacking, b) needing
14	*silly* foolish
15	*tender* feel tenderly towards
18	*But ... turns* but mothers' advice directs daughters' choices
19	*want* a) need, b) lack
20-21	*And* but
	course of time ... loins I am too old to have any more children.
25	*fain* willingly
31	*zeal you bare* ardent love you bore
	quondam former
33	*censure* advise
35	*jointure* dowry
39	*unpartial* unbiased
	censure judgement
42	*indubitate* undoubted
44	*loose the prison of your life* release your life from its imprisonment (by letting you die)
51	*Albion* Great Britain (from the Latin albus, meaning white – the colour of the cliffs of Dover)
54	*sort* agree
57	*motion* propose
62	*But ... hears* but listens to none of them because of her biased

inclinations

59-60	*vows … allows* vows she won't have a monarch unless she loves him
61	*solicited* courted
62	*beguile* deceive
65-6	*And so … cease* and thus establish a peace so perfect that the power of fortune will never be strong enough to bring it to an end
81	*vantage* advantage
88	*policy* crafty device
89	*Brittany* given Leir's later concern to marry her to the King of Hibernia (Ireland), 1.2.43, it is clear that Brittany here is a variant of 'Britain' probably so spelt to provide the three syllables necessary for the meter.
90	*bewray* betray
	secrecy secret

1.2

2	*peat* a word of uncertain origin; when found in combination with 'proud', it is a term of reproach for a woman.
3	*So slightly … us* to value us so little
5	*quaint device* ingeniously-made trinket
	soon quickly
6	*invention* devising
9	*nice* refined
10	*precise* scrupulous
17	*prick and praise* prick was the bull's-eye or mark aimed at by archers; the phrase 'prick and praise' was common for 'goal'.
20	*hap* chance
22	*whenas* when
24	*Though … disgrace* however much to our disgrace it be
27	*in his shirt* in his night clothes
28	*I have made half a grant already* I have half said yes
31	*import* signify
36	*I am with child until you utter it* I am bursting to know (literally 'I am

	pregnant until you tell me').
39	*out of hand* at once
44	*But … will consent* but he fears she will not consent without great difficulty
49	*so* if
53	*which of you three do* now a grammatical irregularity (we would say 'does' rather than 'do'), but fairly standard practice in early modern English
56	*presently* immediately
58	*look whose* whatever person's
65	*enjoin* direct
75-6	*our revenge … in us* the revenge we will inflict on her will be attributed to piety in us
81	*For why* because
90	*Apollo* the Greek sun-god, patron of music, poetry, medicine and archery
	Jove another name for the Roman chief-god Jupiter
97	*aggravate* exacerbate

1.3

8	*regard* concern
11	*watch* keep awake
12	*wantons* unruly children
	toys amusements
17	*affords* yields
	conformable compliant
18	*presageth* forecasts
21	*present* immediate
23	*tenor* drift
30	*assizes* court sessions, here 'judgement day'
31	*tender* cherish
36	*their* a grammatical irregularity, but not unusual in early modern English

	hest bidding
40	*rehears'd* related
50	*vassal* base person, slave
60-61	*And never … forwardness* and can only be quenched by an attempt to show the same outwardly
66	*case* instance
68	*mean* means
71	*haply* perhaps
74	*Philomel* nightingale (from Philomela who, according to the classical myth, changed into a nightingale when Tereus, her rapist, tried to kill her)
78	*paint … forth* give pretend colour to; putting on make-up was called 'painting'.
80	*look what* whatever
83	*brook* put up with; Leir here casts doubt on Cordella's legitimacy.
85	*slight* weak
86	*minion* darling, favourite, but here used in a contemptuous sense
87	*peremptory* imperious
90	*Their* a grammatical irregularity, but not unusual in early modern English
97	*foster thee to this* bring you up to this point in your career
108	*But … far off* but other people who agree with you do not seem to be around
113	*issue* child
114	*tittle* the smallest jot; literally a tittle is a small stroke in handwriting
120	*dower* dowry
122	*This done, because* when I have done this, so that
123	*part* portion
125	*presently* immediately
127	*plain-dealing* straightforward
	sheen bright, shining
129	*Now 'whither, poor forsaken, shall I go'* Probably a line from a popular song: the same phrasing is also found Samuel Daniel's *To Delia*

(1592), Sonnet 52.
135   *lord thus fond* lord so foolish as
138   *tenor* drift

2.1

3   *flying fame* speedy rumour
4   *prodigal* extravagant
7   *allow of* agree with
8   *Venus* the Goddess of love
11   *Jason* leader of the Argonauts who went on a perilous journey to
       find the golden fleece
13   *beseeming* befitting
23   *enjoin* direct, command
25   *so that* provided that
29   *congés* French word meaning salutations or gestures of respect
34   *mean* way
42   *palmers' weeds* pilgrim's clothes. Technically a palmer was a pilgrim
       who had been to the holy land, and carried a palm to prove the fact.
43   *mistrust* be suspicious of
44   *fit your turn* meet your requirements
45   *kin to the Blunts* possibly because Mumford is a variant of
       Mountford: 'The great Elizabethan family of the Blounts enjoyed
       the baronial title of Mountjoy, to which a mysterious allusion is
       possibly made there' (Lee, p. xxxv).
48   *pleasant* joking, humorous

2.2

12   *stay* prop
15   *Daedelus* and his son Icarus made a pair of wings out of feathers and
       wax to escape from the Labyrinth of Minos. They took off
       successfully, but when Icarus flew too close to the sun, the wax
       melted, and he fell into the sea where he drowned.
17   *Troynovant* London. This title, meaning 'new Troy' reflected the

false belief that the city's first king had been 'Trojan Brutus', the grandson of Aeneas of Troy.

25   *slenderly accompanied* meagrely attended

29   *to break ... circumstances* to stop beating about the bush

30   *brook* endure

38   *moiety of half his regiment* share of half his kingdom; possibly 'of' is a misprint for 'or' (a suggestion made in the Malone Society Reprint)

42   *we ... call* we must call each other brothers-in-law

46   *seignories* domains

47-48   *Whom ... part* I would gladly have accepted Ragan even if only a third of the land were offered.

48   *complements* qualities

50   *'Sblood* by God's blood – a common expletive

51-2   *whole/hole* a double entendre: 'whole', here, means all; and 'hole', vagina

62   *For ... intent* for fear that our delay may alter his intended purpose of dividing the kingdom

2.3

3   *sir-reverence* from 'salva reverentia', saving your reverence

5   *Since time* from this time
      warn'd ordered

10   *reclaim'd again* reversed in his decision

15   *Beshrew* curse; 'you've put your finger on it'

20   *She ... wife* This might be a line from a song. A manuscript note against this line in the British Museum copy of the play reads '† the second part / to the same Tune'.

22-23   *nothing* the same double entendre that Hamlet makes (*Hamlet*, 3.2.128) where 'nothing' means no 'thing': no penis.

25   *I cry you mercy* I beg your pardon

27   *benefice* a church living

27   *She'll lay ... back* 'she'll put her husband's ecclesiastical income on her back' i.e. she'll spend his money on clothes.

31   *I think long* I grow impatient
36   *sue* plead
43   *kind* loving (with the added sense of 'related by kinship')
        pelican an emblem of parental devotion; it was thought that a
        mother pelican would offer her own blood to feed her starving
        young.
46   *dazzle* overpower with strong light
45-7   the eagle was said to test her young by forcing them to look into the
        sun. Those whose eyes watered were killed.
53   *Priam* the last king of Troy, had fifty sons and many daughters.
        During the Trojan war, he bravely entered the Greek camp in order
        to beg Achilles for the body of his son Hector. N.B. Another of his
        sons, Paris, was responsible for the Trojan war in the first place.
55   *for that* because
65   *Leander to Hero* Leander swam the Hellespont every night to visit
        his lover Hero. N.B. But when he drowned in a storm one night,
        Hero killed herself.
66   *Aeneas and the Carthage Queen* Aeneas was the hero of Virgil's poem
        The Aeneid. Dido, queen of Carthage, fell in love with him. N.B.
        But when Aeneas left Dido to pursue his destiny in Italy, she threw
        herself onto a burning pyre and died.
68   *no worse than his* an ambiguous statement: his (Aeneas') political fate
        was to become the founder of Rome; his amorous fate was to drive
        his lover Dido to suicide.
78   *resteth* remains
83   *erst* at first
86   *sojourn* reside for a time
87   *beads* rosary
99   *an if* if

                                    2.4

1   *brook* endure
2   *told you of* warned you about

7	*Zounds* by God's wounds – a common expletive
13	*Jack* a diminutive for John, often used for a fool or knave; 'Well' in this sentence is probably pronounced 'will'.
20	*queen of chance* i.e. Fortune
21	*pattern* example
23	*brunts* assaults
28	*willingly ... the rod* she gladly embraces the thing that makes her suffer (a religious commonplace, especially for women)
32	*habit* attire
38	*Oh brave!* Bravo!
39	*Saint Denis* the patron saint of France
	sadly solemnly
45	*'Sblood* by God's blood – a common expletive
	seamster seamstress
48	*get in* (to the labyrinth) with obvious double entendre
49	*cross* oppose
50	*try* test
53	*vouchsafe* grant
59	*silly* weak
59-60	*mouse ... lion* refers to Aesop's story of the lion released from the hunter's net by a mouse
61	*defer'st* submits
63	*hapless* luckless
65	*debar* prevent
75	a metrically defective line, possibly missing a 'that': 'Sweet lady, say [that] there should come a king'.
80	*spoil* despoil i.e. deprive
81	*interest in my mind* claim in my judgement
83	*sue* plead, supplicate
84	*Except* unless
92	*lusty* healthy, vigorous
94	*crave* beg
95	*Hymen* the Greek god of marriage; marriage itself

101   *whilom* some time ago
102   *postulate* demand
104   *Hath light on me* have alighted on me; it was not unusual in
        Elizabethan grammar for a singular verb to have a plural subject.
105   *Surcease* end
106   *whereas* in which
113   *straight* strict
126   *cordial* a pick-me-up which revives and comforts the heart; here
        also a pun on Cordella's name.
131   *slenderly accompanied* with very few servants
132   *vassal* servant
139   *sparks* the animating principles in man; those qualities of a person
        that cannot be disguised.
140   *weeds* garments
147   *foppets* foolish people
        except unless
149   *resteth* remains
157   *except* unless
159   *humour* mood

3.1
14   *in ... sort* in a very shameful manner
15   *dotard* an imbecile
17   *wise* manner
18   *vild* vile
19   *contemned of* held in contempt by
20   *restrain'd* withheld
26   *counsel* advise
29   *latest* last

3.2
2   *dignity* high rank
3   *peremptory* imperious

4	*doting* senile stupidity or foolish affection
5	*I him keep of alms* I provide for him
7	*our* the royal plural
8	*To check and snap me up* to reprimand me and speak sharply to me
11	*doltish* foolish
12	*senseless check* unnecessary reprimand
15	*captious* disposed to find fault
23	*still* continually
30	*for why* because

3.3

2	*frolic* make merry
	were wont used to
13	*dumps* low spirits
17	*I'll provide … cheese* I'll punish him with peasant fare.
24	*partial* biased
26	*weigh* estimate
27	*she breeds young bones* she is pregnant
30	*belike* in all likelihood
35	*go pack* go off, go away
38	*'Tis wrested straight* it's immediately twisted
41	*else* otherwise
45	*wight* human-being
49	*disconsolate* distress
52	a metrically defective line, possibly missing the word 'king': 'Upon the worthless state of old [king] Leir'.
55	*how ill art thou advis'd* how injudicious you are
59	*want* need
60	*recompense* reward, repay
64	*excrement* refuse, faeces
70	*I still enjoyed my own* I continued to be happy in my own rank.
72	*due revenues* income rightly given to you
80	*confute* disprove, refute

103   *entreat* treat
104   *practise* devise a means

3.4

2   *Which bodeth unto me* which foretells to me
3   *vouchsafes* promises
10   *wanteth* lacks
11   *cooling card* a term from a now forgotten game, used to mean anything that 'cools' someone's passion or enthusiasm.
12   *gall* bile or any intensely bitter substance
13   *quartermaster* a petty officer who attends to the steering of the ship, perhaps here with the meaning of 'part-ruler'.

3.5

2   *sequester'd* set aside, separated
10   *whom ... longest home* whom sorrow would have brought to her grave
13   *At unawares* secretly
18   *be frolic* be happy
21   *post* man with a horse who carries letters or messages
30   *haply* by chance
33   *to-do* ado
51   *neck-verse* a Latin verse given to convicts. Prisoners unable to read the text were often hanged by the secular court; prisoners able to read it could claim 'benefit of clergy' and be tried by the (often more lenient) ecclesiastical court.
55   *truss'd up* tied up
59   *we ... thee* we have a high regard for you
60   *surfeit* feed to excess, feast, revel
67   *tripes* intestines, guts etc; hence paunch
70   *scavenger* collector of filth, street-cleaner
75   *forfeiture* penalty
77   *oyster-wife* a woman who sells oysters

78   *Billingsgate* the name both for a gate into the city of London, and for the fish-market that flanked it. Bad language, frequently spoken there, came itself to be known as 'billingsgate'.

82   *choler* anger (and the yellow bile, one of the four bodily humours, thought to have caused it)

83   *razor of Palermo* appears to mean 'razor of the best quality', though the reasons for this are obscure

92   *detracted* disparaged

95   *commons* common people

103   *conceit it is already done* think it is already done

105   *as a poulter leaves a cony* as a poulterer (dealer in dead fowls and game) leaves a rabbit

110   *make him away* kill him

114   *presently* immediately

4.1

6   *whenas* when

13-14 *I cannot ... may have* if I wish for anything I need, or if I lack anything, I can have it.

18   *pine* starve

30   *charity* love

4.2

1   *stay yourself* support yourself

4   a metrically defective line, possibly missing an 'art': 'Thou art as old as I, but [art] more kind'.

9   *tireful* tiring

12   *guerdon* reward

14   *these kind words, which cuts my heart in two ...* It was not unusual in Elizabethan grammar for a singular verb to have a plural subject.

15   *want* lack

21   *whereas* where

23   *gratify* reward, requite

25	*heavy* grievous
31	*of force* of necessity
35	*endurable* unendurable
36	*disaster chance* disastrous occasion
37	*spare* thin
41	*whence springs the ground* what is the cause
44	*finger in the eye* crying
49	*whenas* when
51	*doting* showing the foolishness of age
53	*upon a spleen* for reasons of ill-humour (the spleen was thought to be the seat of anger and melancholy)
55	*to be moan'd and made on* to be cooed to and fussed over

4.3

17	*dumb-show* wordless gestures, the part of a play given over to action without speech
19	*crowns* coins worth five shillings each
23	*give out* proclaim
24	*list* like
27	*take good heed* pay good attention
32	*commons* common people
34	*call'd in question for his fact* questioned about his actions
35	*upon that occasion* for that reason
36	*stealing* creeping
41	*cavillations* trifling objections, from the Latin cavallari ('to practise jesting')
	my state my land, my situation
53	*compact* composed
	adamant a name applied to hard substances; an imaginary rock so hard as to be entirely unbreakable
61	*we* Ragan here breaks into the royal 'we'
68	*stab* used here with a sexual connotation

4.4

13	*stock* tree-trunk
14	*sere* dry, shrivelled
15	*thou … stock* your 'branch' has been grafted onto another tree
24	*unkindly* contrary to the laws of 'kind' or kindred – so, lacking in filial affection or respect
29-30	*Not that I miss … Doth* i.e. The fact that I miss … does not
37	*stay themselves* suspend themselves
38	*element* sky
46	*phoenix* paragon – literally refers to the mythical bird of gorgeous plumage, who never dies
50	*whereas* where
55	*suffice the turn* serve the purpose
56	*half of all my crown* offer to share the management of the country with him
60	*erst* formerly
62	*remunerate* recompense

4.5

1	*It is a world* it is a marvel
	flush well supplied (with money)
3	*seeks* a plural subject with a singular verb
9	*and it like* if it please
13	*dispatch'd* completed
15	*right strange consequence* very odd matter
36	*so* if
47	*mistrust* suspect
50	*indictment* formal accusation
54-55	*pipe … Argus* Argus' hundred eyes, set to watch Io, were put to sleep when Mercury, the messenger of the gods, played on his reed-pipe.
58	*dispatch'd* completed (the task)
59	*I'll find … after him* I'll find a way to kill you

4.6

1	*stay* linger
2	*so long since* such a long time ago
5	*dally* trifle with – with pun on 'delay'
13	*An't* if it
16-17	*Is not … Gone thither* perhaps your father's gone there
20	salutes plural subject with singular verb
36	*I had … to himself* I was commanded to give it to him
38	*brook* endure
48	*until* up to
57	*expiate* to appease, avert
59	*exasperate* aggravate
62	*misconceiv'd* erroneously thought
72	*cross* thwart

4.7

2	*'Tis news* it is a novelty
	rathe early
3	*heavy* sleepy
6	*use to do* usually do
10	*'good fellows'* robbers
12	*we were in good case for to answer them* we'd be in a fine position to fight them (the statement is ironic)
13	*'Twere not for us to stand upon our hands* that's not something to concern ourselves about
14	*scant* scarcely
15	*how* what
16	*Ev'n* just
17	*ill hap* bad fortune
19	*heavy* sleepy
22	*rob-thief* and rob him, the thief
	perforce by force

25	*to-do* ado
37	*Mass* By the Mass – a common expletive
39	*marvel* wonder
41	*miscarry* come to harm, perish
43	*amazeth* panics
45	*slight* trifling
48	*effect* drift
49	*pretends* signifies
52	*aspects* faces
53	*falchion* short slightly curved sword
55	*poniard* dagger
58	*balsam* aromatic medicine for healing wounds
62	*erst* formerly
64	*yet* still
65	*presently* immediately
67	*with much ado* with great difficulty
68-9	*deliver* a pun on deliver meaning 'hand over', and deliver meaning 'set free'
73	*halberds* long-shafted weapons with axe-like heads and hooks on the reverse side, here used ironically – the only 'weapons' Leir and Perillus have are their books.
74	*want* lack
76	*stay* endurance
77	*watch* be awake
78	*proper* comely
79	*'Sblood* by God's blood – a common expletive
80	*belike* perhaps
85	*wish* I wish
89	*use me* employ me or my name to your advantage
90	*pleasure* please
98	*for a vantage* to try to get an advantage over him
99	*try this gear* test this nonsense ('gear' meant matter or 'stuff')
105	*Prithee* please (a corruption of 'I pray thee')

120	*Damon* loyal friend. When Pythias was condemned to death, Damon pledged his life for him.
123	*mortal* living (literally, capable of dying)
126	*final period* an end point, a full-stop
130	*Zounds* by God's wounds – a common expletive
133	*apparel* clothes
	Sirrah Sir
134	*fashion* appearance
140	*see* singular subject, plural verb, a grammatical irregularity not unusual in early modern English
144	*ire* anger
155	*heinous* outrageously wicked
158	*except* aside
159	*doting* foolish, affectionate
160	*heaven's bright eye* the sun
162	*thou dost mistake the mark* you are shooting wide of the target, you are mistaken
169-70	*thou art … the world* the whole world is in love with you
170	*but now* even now
171	*issue* children
172	*t'abridge thy fate* to curtail your future (to kill you)
173	*fie* an exclamation, originating from an imitation of the sound instinctively made when sniffing something disagreeable
177	*doomsday* the day of judgement, when God decides the fate of everyone who ever lived
186	*heinous* outrageously wicked
198	a metrically defective line, possibly missing a 'nor': 'Then neither heav'n, [nor] earth, nor hell be witness …'
200	*prosecute* continue
202	*crack my credit* damage my reputation / damage my financial relationship
204	*Jehovah* Yahweh, the name of God as revealed to Moses
222	*latest* last

225	*withal* thereupon
	desire request
228	*charity* love
230	*errand* message
237	*presently* immediately
239	*ride post* 'take the post-horse' i.e. go quickly
246	*It skilleth not* it doesn't matter
	whit the least bit
248	*Marry* Indeed! Forsooth! (from 'By Mary')
250	*proper* handsome
	Rife plentiful
252	*the high anointed of the Lord* refers to the belief that kings were appointed by God as His deputies on earth, and ruled by 'divine right'
253	*be advised* consider
265	*miscarry* come to harm
286	*incense* provoke
297	*continue* prolong
298	*Why stay'st thou* why do you pause
302	*Beshrew you* curse you!
303	*parlousest* most cunning, mischievous
306	*why the case so stands* why the situation is as it is
309	*It shall go hard but I will thee re-greet* I'll salute you unless prevented by overpowering difficulties.
311	*hie us* hasten ourselves
319	*succour* relieve, help
325	*charity* love
327	*What time* when
334	*tried* tested

4.8

3	*hie me thither presently* hurry there immediately
11	*fain* gladly

13   *hop without her hope* she'll have to proceed with her hope unfulfilled.
14   *want* lack
16   *post* hurry

5.1

1   *by this* by now
3   *my mind presageth* my mind foretells
8   *The last means helps, if that we miss the first* if the first attempt doesn't work, the next will.
14   *maid* virgin
16   *at all adventures* at any risk
17   *well put in* well interposed – but Mumford understands it in its sexual meaning
24   *proper* attractive
25   *do more than she would do* do more than she intends
26   *I have a pair of slops for the nonce* I have a pair of baggy stockings for the occasion.
28   *hose* stockings
30   *bobs* taunts
31   *bombast* cotton-wool used as a padding for clothes; by extension the word came to mean inflated or turgid language, 'tall talk'
37   *serve the turn* answer the purpose
37-8   refers to the practice of carting prostitutes through the street as punishment
48   *very now* precisely now
       go in progress travel
50   *motion* excitement
52   *let this match go forward* let this contest go on
54   *needs not* is unnecessary
55   *so* if
68   *'Twere more than time* it's about time
       device contrivance
69   *let us about it!* Let us set about doing it

5.2

5	*light horse* lightly armed cavalry
6	*regiment* kingdom
7	*post* messenger on a horse
12	*counterfeit* false, copied
22	*moves this innovation* brings about this new situation
23	*timeless* prematurely
31	*heinous* wicked
32	*Censure* judge
38	*This matter shall be sifted* this issue shall be scrutinized ('to sift' is literally to pass something through a sieve).
47	*import* convey
52	*There is good packing* there is good plotting or intrigue
57	*colour* paint over, disguise
64	*slight* flimsy
66	*law of arms* 'diplomatic immunity' for the representative of another government forbidding mistreatment of that person
70	*no whit* not a jot
76	*tender* offer
81	*enforce* press home, emphasize
82	*doubtful* full of doubts, doubting
86	*saucy mate* rude fellow
97	*obloquy* disgrace
104	*parricide* father-killing
106	*admire* marvel at
108	*prosecute* carry out, exact

5.3

4	*want* lack
5	*'good fellows'* robbers
9	*wanting* lacking
	use the mean find a means, contrive

13	*marvel* wonder
14	*room* place
15	*though ne'er so mean* no matter how inferior you are
16-17	*I'll not stand to do* I'll not hold off doing
17-18	*motley gaberdine* parti-coloured smock
20	*I'll forgive your passage* I'll let you off payment for the cost of your passage
22	*match* bargain
24	*sheep's russet sea-gown* a reddish-brown woollen sea-gown
	bide more stress withstand more strain
26	*change* exchange
32	*doublet* close-fitting upper-body garment, the precursor to the jacket
34	*powder'd beef* preserved beef
35	*can of good liquor* 'can' denoted a vessel of any material used for holding liquids
37	*the best is* the best thing/point/circumstance is [that]
41	*do fit* are fitting
46	*I'll use … as another* I'll cheat you as I would anyone else
54	*serve our turns* answer our purposes
58	*or ever* before
61	*henbane* the common name for Hyoscyamus niger, a noxious and poisonous plant
	mithridate a pleasant tasting substance made from many ingredients and thought to be a universal antidote against poison and infectious diseases. It was named after King Mithridates VI of Pontus, who supposedly rendered himself proof against poisons by constantly taking antidotes.
62	*wormwood* Artemisia absinthium, proverbial for its bitter taste
70	*ire* wrath
	respectless disrespectful
71	*paps* breasts
75	*go aslope* go askew

78	*vessel* drinking cup
86	*crosses* vexations, misfortunes
96	*ill apaid* badly requited

5.4

6	*whenas we happ'd* when we happened
11	*quirks* peculiar behaviour
	to beyond the moon to go to ridiculous lengths
12	*And so take on them with such antic fits* and so they assume such bizarre behaviour
16	*make myself fat* a common phrase to describe the process of laughing
18	*o'ergone* overcome
28	*betide unto* befall
35	*virtue* strengthening, sustaining, or healing properties
64	*occasion* reason
71	*ground* reason
89	*present* immediate
90	a metrically defective line, possibly missing an 'a': 'I warrant he ne'er stays to say [a] grace'.
93	*folk* folk's
96	*Aeson* father of Jason, leader of the Argonauts, who was restored to youthfulness by a potion given him by Medea
99	*Elias* Elijah the prophet who 'did eat and drink, and went in the strength of that meat forty days and forty nights unto Horeb the mount of God', 1 Kings 19.8.
105	*forsake their office* leave of performing their function
109-10	*blessed manna … the Israelites* when the Israelites were making their progress through the Wilderness (Exodus 16), God sent down divine 'bread from heaven', called 'manna', to sustain them
113	*congratulate* express our gratitude
116	*requital* recompense
121	*strange and unacquainted men* people who are strangers not acquaintances

123	*occasion* reason
127	*owe* own
129	*interest* credit / legal right
134	*as him list* as he wants
136	*I have … I had* I have two more daughters than I wish I had
141	*adamant* an imaginary rock that was so hard as to be entirely unbreakable
148	*sped* provided, furnished
157	*vild* vile – old spelling has been kept here to preserve the rhyme
164	*mark* note
165	*sojourn'd* resided for a while
166	*entreated* treated
173	*contumelious* insolent
175	*fain … to repair* glad to go
178	*sore* severe
180	*betime* early
182	*pointing* appointing
183	*shag-hair'd* literally someone with shaggy or matted hair; often used as a term of abuse meaning 'ruffian'
191	*censure* critical judgement
210	*resign'd* given over
211	*the word beseems not me* it is unseemly for me to use the word ('pardon')
217	*whenas* when
226	*respective* respectful
232-33	The blessing is in Genesis 12.2-3: 'I will make you a great nation; I will bless you And make your name great; And you shall be a blessing. I will bless those who bless you, And I will curse him who curses you; And in you all the families of the earth shall be blessed.
239	*hap* fortune
259	*gelded* emasculated, castrated

5.5

2	*fact* action
7	*for to* in order to
12	*manifest* broadcast
13	*white-liver'd* having livers lacking in bile – so without courage or spirit
17	*nothing but mere pity* no more than pitiful
20	*brave* courageous
22	*heartless* cowardly
23	*a pox on them!* Curse them! Pox was an all-purpose name for diseases characterized by 'pocks' or pustules; it often refers specifically to syphilis.
24	*paltry* worthless
29	*as good a shift as I can for one* devise as good a stratagem as possible for me
30	*repines* complains

5.6

2	*whereas* where
8	*Truth and justice fighteth on our sides* plural subject, singular verb – a common grammatical irregularity in early modern English
11	*wight* fellow
12	*meanest* lowest-ranked
13	*second* support
17	*wonted* usual
23	*hap* fortune
29	*Genovestan Gauls* Gauls from Orléans
30	*Redshanks* a name commonly applied to Irish Celts or Gaelic Scots, who went bare legged; here reused by Mumford to imply 'blood-spattered up to the shanks'.
32	*right* true
34	*gall* bile (but used to describe any intensely bitter substance)

36   *halberd* military weapon that was a kind of combination of spear and
        battle-axe consisting of a sharp-edged blade ending in a spear-head
36   *bills* another word for halberd; here it clearly refers to the top of the
        halberd which terminated in a spear-head.

                                    5.7
5   *fire* light
13   *goodman* host of an inn
14   *bacon* the joke depends on 'beacon' and 'bacon' being pronounced
        the same way.
17   *excuse* 1 Watchman uses the wrong word for 'accuse'
20   *ass* the joke depends on 'as' and 'ass' being pronounced the same
        way.
        By craft by design
26   *half-a-score* ten (a 'score' is twenty)
30   *conster* construe
        presently immediately

                                    5.8
1   *ensigns* banners
11   *assail* attack

                                    5.9
19   *lack* want
21   *in mean space* meantime, meanwhile
        want lack
22   *tall* stout
25   *'A* he
        choler anger
27   *an* if

                                    5.10
3   *revoke your fealty* renounce your allegiance to

8	*so* as long as
9	*perforce* of necessity
18	*for to* in order to
	their refers to Gonoril, Ragan, Cornwall and Cambria
20	*apace* quickly
23	*adventur'd* risked
27	*wont* accustomed
30	*want* lack
33	*have the foil* be repulsed
35	*prosecute* pursue
36	*Methinks* it seems to me
	amplify enlarge in capacity
39	*Saint Denis* patron saint of France
42	*perforce* through force
48	*fell* ruthless, savage
56	*Except* unless
	fly rush
58	*ferret* hunt
59	*crake* to make a harsh noise; the word was often applied to the sound produced by crows and geese.
62	*a colour's sake* a disguise, a pretext
65	*broach* give vent to
68	*Puritan* technically a member of a party of English Protestants who regarded the reformation of the church under Elizabeth as incomplete; the movement was unpopular amongst theatre people and the word is here used to mean 'hypocrite'.
69	*stark naught* absolutely nothing
70	*Anon* as soon as
88	*mean* intend
91	*betimes* early
93	*latter day* last judgement

5.11

6	*in a manner* to a considerable degree
7	*Zounds* by God's wounds – a common expletive
12	*set them* graft them
22	*scathe* hurt
26	*grutch* complain
30	*unkind* ungently, contrary to the laws of 'kind' or kindred
39	*laid on* depended on a hazard, been set at stake
41-2	*Who with … did play* who, together with my daughters, played the fugitives (i.e. ran away) in order to save their lives

SYNOPSIS

The ageing Leir resolves, in the absence of male heirs, to divide his crown between his three daughters, Gonoril, Ragan and Cordella. But he decides first to marry his daughters to neighbouring British kings. Cornwall and Cambria, he knows, are interested in Gonoril and Ragan, but Cordella has declared she will not marry without love. Leir hatches a plan to ask which of his daughters loves him most (an idea suggested by his counsellor Scaliger): he intends to make Cordella prove her love to him by taking up his choice of husband. Scaliger tells Gonoril and Ragan Leir's plan; the two women, jealous of Cordella's attractions, plot to tell their father they love him so much they will marry anyone he chooses. They do so. By comparison Cordella tells Leir she loves him as a child should – and he is furious. He decides to divide his kingdom between Cordella's two sisters.

The King of Gallia and his comic side-kick Mumford dress as pilgrims and sail to Britain having heard that the country is full of beautiful women. On arrival, they overhear Cordella complaining of her misfortune. She and Gallia fall in love and decide to marry.

At Leir's palace, Cornwall and Cambria draw lots for the two halves of the kingdom. That done, Leir leaves to live with Cornwall and Gonoril – but Gonoril is exasperated by her father's unwanted advice and Scaliger suggests she halve Leir's allowance to make him feel unwelcome. Leir and Gonoril quarrel; he realises his daughter wishes him dead. Comforted by his friend Perillus, he sets off to stay with Ragan. Cornwall, worried about Leir's welfare, sends a Messenger after him. But Gonoril intercepts the Messenger, and replaces Cornwall's letters with letters of her own. When Leir and Perillus arrive at Regan's palace, she has already decided to kill the two old men on the strength of her sister's letters. She tricks Leir and Perillus into meeting her in a secluded place; in fact, only the murderous Messenger is there, whom Leir assumes must have been sent by a vengeful Cordella. But he then learns that his other daughters, Gonoril and Regan, have arranged his death. The old men – with the help of some heavenly thunderclaps – persuade the messenger to relent. On Perillus' advice, Leir goes to find Cordella in France.

Cordella is grief-stricken not to be reconciled with her father. To cheer her up, Gallia sends an Ambassador to England on her behalf – and when the Ambassador reaches Cornwall's place, Gonoril reveals her actual character to him by her double-talk. He is then mistreated by Ragan, who also persuades her husband that Cordella is behind Leir's sudden disappearance. Hearing of the Ambassador's treatment, Cordella, Gallia and Mumford go to find Leir.

Leir and Perillus arrive starving in France where Gallia and Cordella bump into them. Cordella feeds the old men before revealing who she is. They all kneel to ask each other's forgiveness. Then Gallia gathers an army and returns to fight Leir's cause in England. He conquers the first town he reaches because the watchmen who should have been guarding the warning-beacon there are drunk. He and Leir together enter the battlefield where they confront Gonoril and Regan. Leir is victorious and regains his lands; he gives them to Gallia and Cordella as recompense.

TEXTUAL NOTES

King Leir was published anonymously in quarto form in 1605. Only four known copies of that edition survive, two in the British Library, one in the Huntington, and one in the Folger. The Malone Society Reprint [MSR] edition of *Leir*, prepared by W. W. Greg and checked by R. Warwick Bond (Oxford: Oxford University Press, 1908), collates two of the quartos and provides the copytext for this edition; press variants are also taken from that text. Seven other editions of *Leir* have been consulted. They are, in chronological order, *Six Old Plays* vol. 2, selected by George Steevens, ed. by John Nichols (London: S. Leacroft, 1779); *The True Chronicle History of King Leir*, ed. A. F. Hopkinson (1895); *Shakespeare's Library* vol. 6, ed. J. P. Collier, rev. ed. W. C. Hazlitt (London: Reeves and Turner, 1875); *The Chronicle History of King Leir*, ed. Sidney Lee (London: Chatto & Windus, 1909); *Quellen zu Konig Lear*, ed. Rudolf Fischer (Bonn: A. Marcus u. E. Weber, 1914); *Narrative and Dramatic Sources of Shakespeare*, vol. 7, ed. Geoffrey Bullough (London: Routledge and Kegan Paul, 1973); *A Critical Edition of The True Chronicle History of King Leir* ... ed. Donald M. Michie (New York and London: Garland Publishing, 1991).

The following notes record all verbal emendations made to the text, speech prefixes (SPs) and stage directions (SDs). One SP has been changed throughout – The King of Gallia, called 'King' in the quarto, is 'Gallia' in this text to avoid confusion with Leir. SDs of editorial origin are in square brackets in the text, SDs that are lightly rewritten but not substantially changed are recorded in full in the notes. Readings and verbal contractions first suggested by this edition are designated *this edn*; others are attributed to the edition that first suggested them. The quarto provides no act or scene divisions, although it opens 'Actus I'; act and scene divisions here are taken from Lee. Modernisation has been as thorough as possible. 'Indure' has been rendered 'endure', perfit – perfect, then – than (where appropriate), shipwrack – shipwreck, murtherer – murderer, I – aye, jointer – jointure, vild – vile. On two occasions (3.1.18 and 5.4.157), old spelling has been retained for a rhyming couplet. Modernisation has caused some difficulty when presenting jokes based on words that were once homophones (words that are different in meaning but sound the same), significantly 'beacon' and 'bacon', 'ass' and 'as'. Both spellings have been used in the text, and explained in the glossarial notes.

The quarto is printed as though almost the whole text is in verse. But some speeches, particularly comic ones, are either in very loose verse or prose. Where necessary, the verse lining of the quarto has been altered, but the original line endings are provided in the textual notes.

The final 'ed' for verbs in the past tense is rendered –'d when it is not syllabic (and should not be spoken) and –ed when it is (and should be spoken). Several other contractions are provided by the quarto and reproduced here; additional contractions made for the sake of the verse can be found in the notes.

SDs are referred to by the number of the line in which they appear; those that are positioned between spoken lines are indicated by the act, scene and line number that precedes the SD followed by a decimal point and a 1 for the first SD, a 2 for the second etc e.g. 2.2.8.1; SDs that occur at the start of a scene are indicated by act and scene numbers followed by 0.1 etc. e.g.1.1.0.1

1.1

	Act 1, scene 1] *this edn;* ACTUS 1 Q
0.1	SD] *this edn; Enter King Leir and Nobles* Q
1	SP] *Steevens;* not in Q
40	from] *this edn;* for Q
41	SP] *Michie;* Nobl. Q
43	sat] *Lee;* set Q
55	heav'nly] *this edn;* heavenly Q
84	lov'st] *this edn;* lovest Q
93	heav'nly] *this edn;* heavenly Q

1.2

15	desp'rate] *this edn;* desperate Q
66	Th'Hibernian] *this edn;* The Hibernian Q
87	suffice] *this edn;* suffice Q

1.3

1-2	realignment *this edn;* set with line-break at daughters Q

2.1

12	Heav'ns] *this edn;* Heavens Q
54	Heav'ns] *this edn;* Heavens Q

2.2

0.1	SD] *this edn; Enter the King of Cornwall and his man booted and spurd, a riding wand, and a letter in his hand* Q
8.0	SD] *this edn; Enter the King of Cambria booted and spurd, and his man with a wand and a letter* Q

8.2	SD] *this edn; He lookes on the letter* Q
22	Sultan] *this edn;* soldan Q
51	'Sblood] *Lee;* Zlood Q

2.3

13	In truth] *Lee;* Intruth Q
35	SD] *this edn; Enter Leir, Perillus and Others* Q
63	heav'ns] *this edn;* heavens Q
81.0	SD] *this edn; Then they draw lots* Q
99	an] *this edn;* and Q
106	SD] *this edn; Exeunt omnes, manet Perillus* Q

2.4

0.1	SD] *this edn; Enter the Gallian King* ...
45	scamster] *this edn;* sempster Q
64	sometime] *this edn;* sometimes Q
70	giv'n] *this edn;* given Q
91	heav'n] *this edn;* heaven Q
155	prose *this edn;* set as verse with line-endings at know/live/ladies/France Q

3.1

0.1	SD] *this edn; Enter Perillus solus* Q

3.2

39	heav'ns] *this edn;* heavens Q

3.3

10	know] *Steevens;* kuow Q
48.0	SD] *this edn; He weeps* Q
85	undone] *Steevens;* undone Q
99	fall'n] *this edn;* fallen Q

3.4

0.1	SD] *this edn; Enter Ragan solus* Q

3.5

12	stol'n] *this edn;* stolen Q
32	'twere] *this edn;* it were Q

33	to-do] *this edn;* to do Q
44.0	SD] *this edn; a letter* Q
49.0	SD] *this edn; She opens them* Q
50-2	prose *this edn;* set as verse with line-endings at stand/be/letters Q
54-6	prose *this edn;* set as verse with line-endings at I/up/him Q
61-2	prose *this edn;* set as verse with line-endings at words, would Q
83	Palermo] *Steevens;* Palerno Q
92	slanderous] *this edn;* slandrous Q
101-2	prose *this edn;* set as verse with line-endings at ever/ thee Q
103-6	prose *this edn;* set as verse with line-endings at done/will/poulter/skin Q
112-13	prose *this edn;* set as verse with line-ending at matter Q
113	SD] *this edn; kisse the paper* Q
83	Palermo] *Steevens;* Palerno Q

4.1

0.1	SD] *this edn; Enter Cordella solus* Q
24	heav'n] *this edn;* heaven Q
30	e'en] *this edn;* even Q

4.2

15	pow'r] *this edn;* power Q
23.0	SD] *this edn; Enter the prince of Cambria ...* Q
31.0	SD] *this edn; She runneth to him, and kneeles downe, saying:* Q
43.0	SD] *this edn; Exeunt, manet Ragan* Q

4.3

0.1	SD] *this edn; Enter Messenger solus* Q
12	SD] *this edn; She opens the letters* Q
13.0	SD] *this edn; She reads the letter ...* Q
16	see] *Steevens;* she Q

4.4

0.1	SD] *this edn; Enter the Gallian King,* Q

4.5

	SD] *this edn; Enter Messenger solus* Q
9	an] *this edn;* and Q
33.0	SD] *this edn; Give him ...* Q

4.6

13   an't] *this edn;* and it Q

4.7

16   e'en] *this edn;* even Q
19.0   SD] *this edn; They fall …* Q
19.1   SD] *this edn; Enter the Messenger or murtherer with …* Q
25   to-do] *this edn;* to do Q
26   SD] *this edn; See them and start* Q
30.0   SD] *this edn; He takes …* Q
38.0   SD] *this edn; They wake …* Q
41   don't] *this edn;* do not Q
49   portends] *this edn;* pretends Q
53   hands] *Lee;* hand Q
66.0   SD] *this edn; They reele* Q
73.0   SD] *this edn; Shew their Bookes* Q
84   e'en] *this edn;* even Q
84.0   SD] *this edn; Take it* Q
86.0   SD] *this edn; Take his, and weygh them both in his hands* Q
88   an] *this edn;* and Q
91.0   SD] *this edn; They proffer …* Q
95.0   SD] *this edn; Proffer …* Q
105   SP] *this edn;* Ambo. Q
120   Damon] *Steevens;* Damion
160   heav'n's] *this edn;* heavens Q
185   heav'n] *this edn;* heaven Q
186   heav'n] *this edn;* heaven Q
187   heav'ns] *this edn;* heavens Q
193   an] *this edn;* an Q
195   e'en] *this edn;* even Q
196   heav'n] *this edn;* heaven Q
205   heav'n's] *this edn;* heavens Q
205.0   SD] *this edn; They bless …*Q
218   e'en] *this edn;* even Q
220   e'en] *this edn;* even Q
239.0   SD] *this edn; Shew a bagge …* Q
272   SD] *this edn; kneele* Q

274	heav'n] *this edn;* heaven Q
294.0	SD] *this edn; It thunders. He quakes ...* Q
294	heav'ns] *this edn;* heavens Q
295.0	SD] *this edn; He lets fall ...* Q
321	th'other] *this edn;* the other Q
328	she] Steevens; se Q

4.8

	SD] *this edn; Enter ... Ambassador solus* Q
9	louring] *this edn;* low'ring Q

5.1

0.1	SD] *this edn; Enter the King and Queene of Gallia ...* Q
11-13	prose *this edn;* set as verse with line-endings at again/wench/forsworn/live Q
18-20	prose *this edn;* set as verse with line-endings at it/days/France Q
21-5	prose *this edn;* set as verse with line-endings at you/she/you/man/do Q
26-7	prose *this edn;* set as verse with line-endings at nonce/mocks Q
39-45	prose *this edn;* set as verse with line-endings at over/diposed/claim/me/me/unkindness Q
47-9	prose *this edn;* set as verse with line-endings at this/now/side/near Q

5.2

15	loss] *Lee;* less Q
30	heav'ns] *this edn;* heavens Q
38	if't] *this edn;* if it Q
49	in's] *this edn;* in his Q
82	doubtful] *Steevens;* do utful Q
86	SD] *this edn; She strikes ...* Q
95	SD] *this edn; Shee weeps* Q

5.3

10.0	SD] *this edn; Looke on Leir* Q
13	SD] *this edn; Looke on Perillus* Q
21.0	SD] *this edn; Leir & he changeth* Q
27	SD] *this edn; Pull off ...* Q
32	thou'lt] *this edn;* thou wilt Q
39	SD] *this edn; Leir to Perillus* Q
42-4	prose *this edn;* set as verse with line-endings at together/anon/well Q

47-8   prose *this edn;* set as verse with line-endings at money/again Q this

5.4

0.1   SD] *this edn; Enter the Gallian King and Queene* ... Q
33.0   SD] *this edn; He strips up* ...Q
56   ensu'th] *this edn;* ensueth Q
57   []lat'ry] *this edn;* flattery Q
59   heav'ns] *this edn;* heavens Q
84   e'en] *this edn;* even Q
85.0   SD] *this edn; She bringeth* ... Q
87.0   SD] *this edn; Perillus takes Leir* ... Q
90-1   prose *this edn;* set as verse with line-ending at grace Q
94.0   SD] *this edn; They eat hungerly* ...Q
119   SD] *this edn; Perillus proffers his dublet: they* ... Q
160   e'en] *this edn;* even Q
204.0   SD] *this edn; She kneeles* Q
206.0   SD] *this edn; he kneeles* Q
209.0   SD] *this edn; he riseth* Q
210.0   SD] *this edn; he kneeles* Q
225.0   SD] *this edn; He riseth* Q
228.0   SD] *this edn; She kneeles* Q
238.0   SD] *this edn; she riseth* Q
249.0   SD] *this edn; he kneeles* Q
256.0   SD] *this edn; Mumford kneeles* Q

5.5

0.1   SD] *this edn; Enter Ragan sola* Q

5.6

0.1   SD] *this edn; Enter the Gallian King* Q
22   eyes] *Lee;* eye Q
29   Cenovestan] *this edn;* Genovestan Q
37   'pointed] *Lee;* pointed Q

5.7

          SP 1 Captain] *this edn;* Captain Q
11   an] *this edn;* and Q
28   much as to] *this edn;* much to Q

5.8

9   portend] *this edn;* pretend Q

5.9

7-8   verse *this edn;* set with line-ending at drink Q
14   SD] *this edn; He drinks* Q
17   SD] *this edn; draw to stab them* Q
19   SD] *this edn; He kicks ...* Q
27   an] *this edn;* and Q

5.10

0.1   SD] *this edn; Enter the Gallian King* Q
25-28   prose *this edn;* set as verse with line-endings at
             so/grace/skirmishes/this/men/women Q
44   sure] *MSR;* sute Q
46   come] *this edn;* came Q
77.0   SD] *this edn; She snatches them ...*Q
95   an] *this edn;* and Q
95-97   prose *this edn;* set as verse with line-endings at morrow/hands/faces/them Q
99   tongues] *this edn;* tongue Q

5.11

0.1   SD] *this edn; Mumford must chase Cambria away: then cease ...*Q
12.2   SD] *this edn; Leir, Perillus, King* Q
15   heav'ns] *this edn;* heavens Q
25   heav'ns] *this edn;* heavens Q

Reduced facsimile of the first page of *The True Chronicle History of King Leir and his three daughters, Gonorill, Ragan and Cordella* (London, 1605) reproduced by kind permission of the British Library (C.34.L.11).

The true Chronicle Hiſtorie of King Leir and his three daughters.

ACTVS I.

Enter King Leir and Nobles.

Hus to our griefe the obſequies performd
Of our (too late) deceaſt and deareſt Queen,
Whoſe ſoule I hope, poſſeſt of heauely ioyes,
Doth ride in triumph 'mogſt the Cherubins;
Let vs requeſt your graue aduice, my Lords,
For the diſpoſing of our princely daughters,
For whom our care is ſpecially imployd,
As nature bindeth to aduaunce their ſtates,
In royall marriage with ſome princely mates :
For wanting now their mothers good aduice,
Vnder whoſe gouernment they haue receyued
A perfit patterne of a vertuous life :
Left as it were a ſhip without a ſterne,
Or ſilly ſheepe without a Paſtors care ;
Although our ſelues doe dearely tender them,
Yet are we ignorant of their affayres :
For fathers beſt do know to gouerne ſonnes;
But daughters ſteps the mothers counſell turnes.
A ſonne we want for to ſucceed our Crowne,
And courſe of time hath cancelled the date
Of further iſſue from our withered loynes:
One foote already hangeth in the graue,
And age hath made deepe furrowes in my face:
The world of me, I of the world am weary,
And I would fayne reſigne theſe earthly cares,
And thinke vpon the welfare of my ſoule :
Which by no better meanes may be eſſeĉted,
Then by reſigning vp the Crowne from me,
In equall dowry to my daughters three.

Skalliger. A worthy care, my Liege, which well declares,
The zeale you bare vnto our *quondam* Queene :
And ſince your Grace hath licenſ'd me to ſpeake,

A 2